THE

Happily Ever After

A MEMOIR OF AN
UNLIKELY ROMANCE NOVELIST

Avi Steinberg

NAN A. TALESE | DOUBLEDAY

NEW YORK

All rights reserved. Published in the United States by Nan A. Talese/
Doubleday, a division of Penguin Random House LLC, New York,
and distributed in Canada by Penguin Random House Canada
Limited, Toronto.

www.nanatalese.com

Doubleday is a registered trademark of Penguin Random House LLC.
Nan A. Talese and the colophon are trademarks of Penguin Random
House LLC.

Jacket image: Original painting by Max Ginsburg
Jacket design by Matt Dorfman

Library of Congress Cataloging-in-Publication Data
Names: Steinberg, Avi, author.
Title: The happily ever after : a memoir of an unlikely romance
novelist / Avi Steinberg.
Description: First edition. | New York : Nan A. Talese/
Doubleday, 2020.
Identifiers: LCCN 2019049254 (print) | LCCN 2019049255 (ebook) |
ISBN 9780385540254 (hardcover) | ISBN 9780385540261 (ebook)
Subjects: LCSH: Romance fiction—Authorship.
Classification: LCC PN171.R66 S74 2020 (print) |
LCC PN171.R66 (ebook) | DDC 809.3/953—dc23
LC record available at https://lccn.loc.gov/2019049254
LC ebook record available at https://lccn.loc.gov/2019049255

MANUFACTURED IN THE UNITED STATES OF AMERICA

1 3 5 7 9 10 8 6 4 2

First Edition

To my A and my Z

Two basic elements comprise every romance novel: a central love story and an emotionally satisfying and optimistic ending.

A Central Love Story: The main plot centers around individuals falling in love and struggling to make the relationship work. A writer can include as many subplots as he/she wants as long as the love story is the main focus of the novel.

An Emotionally Satisfying and Optimistic Ending: In a romance, the lovers who risk and struggle for each other and their relationship are rewarded with emotional justice and unconditional love.

Romance novels may have any tone or style, be set in any place or time, and have varying levels of sensuality— ranging from sweet to extremely hot. These settings and distinctions of plot create specific subgenres within romance fiction.

—ROMANCE WRITERS OF AMERICA'S

DEFINITION OF THE GENRE

PART ONE

On the Train to RT

Society Defined. Near the beginning of the novel, the society that the heroine and hero will confront in their courtship is defined for the reader. This society is in some way flawed; it may be incomplete, superannuated, or corrupt. It always oppresses the heroine and hero.

—PAMELA REGIS, *A NATURAL HISTORY OF THE ROMANCE NOVEL*

Years ago—long before I became Kensington romance author Dana Becker—someone gave me a useful piece of advice. I was working as a librarian in a prison at the time and an older inmate marched up to the circulation desk and slammed a book onto the checkout counter. Even without looking, I knew the book's genre and could also guess its author. This was a person who had read so many Nora Roberts romance novels, and with such ardor, that her prison nickname was "Nora Roberts." Sometimes this pleased her, sometimes she was touchy about it.

"I know what you're thinking," she'd said to me that day. "But if someone's locked up, *you* don't get to judge what they read."

Looking back on it now, I believe she understated her case. For a person who reads in captivity, the stakes can scarcely be higher. For this sort of reader, there is no such thing as mere escapism. An outsider ought to do more than reserve judgment: better to listen closely and to learn from a captive's book decisions.

Consider that prisoner of fate, Anna Karenina. Toward the end of her life, Anna sits on a train, reading by candlelight. She is transported by the images in her jaunty English novel—the kind of novel that Tolstoy himself had mail-ordered by the dozens as he wrote *Anna Karenina*. When we meet Anna on the train, with her ladies' novel in hand, we see her trying, and failing, to match the story's images with her real life.

> When she read how Lady Mary had ridden after the hounds, teased the bride, and astonished everyone by her boldness—she wanted to do it herself. But there was no chance of doing anything; and twisting the smooth paper knife in her little hands, she forced herself to read. The hero of the novel was already almost reaching his English happiness, a baronetcy and an estate, and Anna was feeling a desire to go with him to the estate . . .

But then something strange happens. As Anna falls deeper into her English novel, a wave of shame washes over her so unexpectedly and so suddenly that she is startled. Why? Anna wonders. Why *shame?*

A reader of contemporary romance can relate. Romance readers are constantly shamed. The uncomfortable reading of a book on a train, or plane, is an old trope. Not long ago, romance publishers offered their readers the option of a false book cover, to help hide the contents. I once heard a romance editor at Random House say that she sends her grandmother boxes of the latest romance novels, "but we never discuss it, we never say a word about it." Excluding romance is a good way for a bookshop to be seen as "serious."

Many romance readers have stories of being shamed for their

love of books characterized by the happily-ever-after ending, or, as romance people call it, the HEA. The HEA is mandatory in romance. It is the definition of it, per the laws set forth by the Romance Writers of America (RWA). The HEA is, to romance readers, a nonnegotiable principle, an inalienable right. Anna Karenina's own story, of course, is no HEA. Unlike the heroine of her English ladies' novel, Anna herself does not ride after the hounds. There is neither baron to go with nor any "English happiness" to be had for Anna. She casts herself under an oncoming train—the train that once gave her space to dream is, in the end, what kills her. This is meant as a brutal dramatization of the disconnect between the stories we read in novels and those we live in reality.

When I was in my twenties *Anna Karenina* struck me as not only heartbreaking but, in its portrait-perfect depictions of her character, also rather true to life. To my younger self, this tale also had something of a feminist bent, for its understanding of Anna as a human being and for the mirror it held up to her society. But now, as an adult, it mostly just pisses me off.

Why did Anna have to die? Is that the more realistic conclusion? Or is it a convenient ending for an author bent on proving a theory about Happiness, as formulated in Tolstoy's catchy first sentence: "All happy families are alike; each unhappy family is unhappy in its own way"? This proposition implies that it was the unhappiness of Anna's fate that made her story unique, and thus worth telling to begin with. If happiness is the principle of romance—of the kinds of novels Anna reads—unhappiness, Tolstoy posits, is the principle of the realist social novel (aka The Novel), the kind of book in which Anna is forced to live and to die. And let's be clear about that death: it was entirely the decision of the author. Anna Karenina didn't throw herself under anything. *Tolstoy* threw her under that train. Her death was no suicide.

Nor was the death of Flaubert's Emma Bovary. She was also killed for her sin of reading romances too literally, or, to be more specific, for her belief that the happiness she encountered in her books was something she might partake of in real life. Though the official cause of her death was self-administered arsenic, Flaubert leaves little doubt what really led to Emma's demise: after the suicide, we see a substance, exactly like black ink, vomiting forth continuously from Emma's mouth. The poison was the books, not the arsenic. But the real culprit here, as with *Anna Karenina,* was the author himself: the deadly black substance wasn't the ink of her romances but rather the ink of Flaubert's own pen.

When I think of those stories today, they seem to me less about why Anna Karenina or Emma Bovary ended her life than about why her (male) author decided to kill her. What was it about her choice of reading that so threatened these writers? Why does Don Quixote's fixation on courtly romances lead him to heroic misadventure, but women who try something like that perish in disgrace? Had Jane Austen written Anna Karenina's and Emma Bovary's story, they would surely have met different endings. Would those endings have been less realistic, less of a mirror to society, a lesser artistic statement?

I think about these murdered reader-heroines often because the outlines of their stories crop up so often in daily life. When I hear that stereotypical take, that romance lit is for "desperate housewives" who live in the middle of the country, I think of Emma Bovary, who lived out in the provinces. I think about Anna Karenina every time a woman sitting next to me on a plane apologizes *to me* for her decision to read a romance novel. "It's *not* smutty," one woman assured me, on a flight to San Francisco, as if she were proposing to light a cigar and blow smoke in my face for the duration of the flight, and not what she actually did: quietly read a book in which an exasperated and put-upon woman gets to win for once in her life.

Which is why, when I first set out on my own romance quest, I was so excited to attend the RT convention, or, as it is known, simply RT. At RT there were no apologies made. It was a gathering of celebration and pride. At RT, every year, romance announced its intentions at elaborate balls and swarming author events, and in giant banners as tall as a New Orleans Marriott.

As someone who dwelled within the angsty world of "literary" publishing, I have, on more than one occasion, found myself leaning my head around the corner to see what was happening down the hall at the romance end of the industry, a situation akin to being at a funeral and hearing the strains of a party happening next door.

My first RT brought me to the New Orleans Marriott, and a panel called "BDSM: The Truth Behind the Fiction," which shared a busy time slot with sessions like "Secrets to Maximizing Your Sales" and something called "pitchslap." This session billed itself as "a lively discussion on BDSM in erotic romance with a group of bestselling authors who actually live the lifestyle!"

As promised, the discussion was lively. It was also informative. "The market for kinky stories is more competitive than ever," one of the authors said from the dais. "We've almost overtaken Paranormal!" (This prompted some grumbling in the audience, presumably among the orthodox Paranormalists.) "Authenticity in your kink writing is going to be one of the things that sets you apart," she added. For the next half-hour the three authors detailed what this has meant to their writing.

It's not just the feel of the whip against your skin, it's the emotions it evokes. The first lash means one thing, the fifth means something else. The feel of the whip when it's being run gently over the nape of your neck . . . that chilly coldness . . . that means something else entirely. This gesture also means something different, emotionally, before a whipping as opposed to after. Seeing the whip from across the room generates its own singular emotions. The whip itself, the leather, can get hot from a lashing. And what does that evoke? The questions were piling up. ("Get the details and report back!" one of the panelists said.)

Here was one solution to the Life-Literature problem, how our lives and our stories never quite match up, and how we always somehow get stuck in the spaces between. For these particular authors, there was no Life-Literature Problem: they were *living the lifestyle*. Toward the end of the session, one of the panelists sighed deeply and remarked, "It's honestly getting so hard to find good submissives out there," to which a small voice from the back of the conference room was heard to shout back, "I'll be your submissive!" The conference room erupted in cheers.

There was a lot happening at RT. There was much to consider

in that New Orleans Marriott. I would see two women named Cherry exchange business cards. I would see some impressively honest marketing ("I'm already drooling over this one," read one blurb). I would hear someone publicly declare, "If your character has amnesia, that's a book I'm definitely reading." I would see a large group of women band together and hijack a men's public bathroom. I would learn that "domestic discipline" was in, as a genre. I would be nodded to knowingly by another male convention-goer, a bald guy with a ponytail down to his lower back, dressed in a Hawaiian shirt and a kilt. I would see well-known cover model CJ Hollenbach and be too lame to say hello. I would on several occasions be told, upon meeting someone, that I was the first Jew they had ever met. I'd be repeatedly cautioned that *Fifty Shades of Grey* should not be regarded as the best example of the Erotica genre, even as these same authors scrambled to learn the marketing lessons of its success. I would meet more people with aliases than I had since I'd worked in prison. And I'd be in the presence of more optimistic writers in a few days than I'd met thus far in my life. That part, in particular, seemed significant to me.

RT was created and run by *RT Book Reviews* magazine, formerly known as *Romantic Times,* which was for many years the paper of record in Romancelandia. Every year since the early 1980s, until its abrupt end in 2019, romance fans would take over a hotel and convention center somewhere in America, to meet authors, attend events and parties, and grab a lot of free books and merch. Authors and industry people went to RT to promote books and to network. Whereas the annual convention of the Romance Writers of America, the RWA, best known for its gala RITA Awards, is a members-only guild meeting, RT was, at its heart, a fan con. For the thousands of readers who made the pilgrimage, year after year, or every few years, as funds permitted, the convention was something you did because you lived for romance. And since so many romance fans were themselves aspiring authors, much of the convention was given to panel discussions on practical matters related to romance writing and marketing. That was why I went that first time.

As luck would have it, I had a guide. My friend Nellie worked at Devon Books, holding a director-level position at one of the biggest names in the industry. Devon is not the real name of the publisher, nor is Nellie the actual name of my friend. But she is real and she is fabulous.

And tough. Once, when she was trying to bully me for some gossip, she told me that she would "cut a bitch" if she didn't get her way immediately. Was it a figure of speech? She'd done it before. When she was in college, at an Ivy League institution that will go unnamed, Nellie used to go around with a knife concealed in her boot. She pulled the shiv on more than one occasion, including once, on a subway train, when she actually stabbed a guy who had been, as she described it, "annoying the shit out of me." At my suggestion that pulling a knife was perhaps an extreme measure, Nellie just shrugged ("It's not like I put it in his *neck* or something").

It is common knowledge in Midtown Manhattan that Nellie is a romance industry dynamo who seems to subsist solely on gummy candy and bestselling books. And when she wasn't busy being fabulous, she enjoyed ridiculing me, especially when she could do so openly to my face, like I was a useless kid brother, a dynamic I found soothingly familiar because it reminded me of my own big sister.

At that first RT, Nellie had already been fully updated about my very recent divorce, courtesy of our mutual friend, Vera, with no juicy details withheld. When we'd met up at the New Orleans Marriott, Nellie already had a wicked look in her eyes, and she was palpably energized by my troubles. She was, as she told me, doubly excited to witness my wretchedness in person, and at a romance convention, of all places ("It's gonna make this whole trip worth it").

When I ran into Nellie outside of a RT session called "Writing Witty Banter," I had been feeling fairly dejected. It was nice to see a familiar face. She approached me eagerly, like she had some news to share. In my weakness, I had interpreted this as excitement to see me.

"Dude," she said to me, with a big smile, "*everyone* here thinks you're a massive pussy!"

"I know," I replied.

"You're not fooling *any*one."

"I'm not trying to fool anyone."

"Yeah: *don't.*"

Nellie's digs tended to have a revelatory quality about them. In introducing me to another romance publisher at RT, for instance, she'd said, "So, okay, he writes these nonfiction books where he, like, joins some group where he isn't welcome? And they end up *haaating* him. It's *hil*arious." It wasn't exactly how I'd ever described my previous work, but it was a devastatingly plausible reading.

Nellie quickly became a romance publishing mentor to me, and I collected and examined her statements. She once told me, as we sat in her office, surrounded by shelves overpacked with Devon romances, "An author can fail with one book. And even a second one. But once your third book fails, we might have to find you a new name." There was a lot behind that statement. And as someone who had published two books, embarking on a third, I was listening carefully.

As for my conversion to romance, Nellie respected it, not because she respected me but because she respected romance. But she was mostly amused by the spectacle I presented.

"Dude, you suck at it," Nellie would tell me. "You know that, right?"

"How do you know that?" I replied. "You haven't read anything I've written."

Nellie burst out laughing.

"Um, yeah," she said. "And I'm definitely not gonna *read* anything you write."

She laughed some more at the very thought of it. "But I wouldn't need to, honestly, to know that you suck at it."

When she saw how genuinely bummed I was getting, she took a moment to relish her triumph before getting annoyed at me for ruining it.

"Ugh, don't get all sad," she said, rolling her eyes. "Obviously *you're* gonna suck at it."

Like so many of Nellie's statements, I grasped this statement as a piece of wisdom, something worth meditating over.

For one thing, it was true. I had a lot to learn. My career as a professional writer helped somewhat, but mostly it gave me the skills to recognize that I lacked the romance chops. In many ways, including just at the technical level, I was out of my element. But I was an eager student. At RT, deep in the heart of the hotel, I furiously took notes at a panel discussion called "Writing Quickly—Tricks and Tips."

Despite the allure of competing conference panels such as "Romance, Bollywood Style," "Worldbuilding for Every Genre," and "Banging Hot Betas," I had to focus on the immediate task before me. I showed up at "Writing Quickly," eager for some of those tricks and tips.

The session was delayed as we awaited the third "Writing Quickly" panelist, who finally ran into the conference room on stockinged feet, panting, holding up her heels and shouting, "I'm here! I'm here! Sorry I'm late. Don't kill me!" This would set the tone. One author on the panel confessed to being on Facebook "all day, every day." Her approach was to alternate twenty-minute-long blocks: twenty minutes writing, twenty minutes Facebooking, twenty writing, twenty Instagramming, etc. To which another panelist replied, "Having more than one name, I've been driven *literally* crazy on social media."

But there was good news, too. "The start of a book is slow," an author pointed out. "But the end vomits itself out. In my experience, at least." (Later that day, another author, on the "Going Hybrid" panel, had similarly testified, "I can fart out novellas.")

From the audience, a studious young woman with an asymmetrical hairdo and giant glasses asked, "How much of your time do you spend plotting?"

The panel, it turned out, was not so into plotting. One of the authors mentioned, however, that when you get to the point where you're thinking about "killing every single character" it might be time to take stock.

The "Writing Quickly" panelists, three bestselling romance authors, spent much of the conversation discussing their daily word counts. Needless to say, these word counts were sensational. One of the authors said she pumps out a chapter a day, seven days a week; she can complete a book every two months. She currently works with six different publishers, in addition to self-pubbing. "And . . . I've got dogs and a husband," she said, with a sigh.

Though she likes Historicals, she advises the rushing writer to work in other genres: less research, more time to write. Later in the discussion, when the conversation turned to "the challenges of being prolific," she told the standing-room crowd of romancers and hopefuls, "You *will* gain weight." And, she added, "You see me rubbing my neck up here? My shoulder is as hard as a rock." She has a pinched nerve, she said. She's cried at a massage therapist. More alarming: she's made a massage therapist cry. She's written romances from hospital beds. I looked around the room. People were hunched over, silently scribbling notes.

The other panelists, it turned out, wrote at an even greater clip. One of the authors, a former history professor who plots "only as much as can fit on a Panera napkin," works in the Erotic, Paranormal, Contemporary, and Fantasy genres. She also writes

Romantic Suspense and "can't afford to keep the readers waiting too long" with her next installment. Under pressure from a publisher, she once wrote a 100,000-word novel, called *Hard As It Gets,* in under four weeks. ("I used to have a garden; now it's all weeds.") Her five-book Hard Ink series left her with cluster migraines and major weight gain.

The other panelist, a former trial lawyer, who often scribbles at her kids' basketball practice and in school carpool lines, writes at a truly terrifying daily rate that I won't mention yet because it deserves a complete sentence of its own. Ten thousand words a day. This figure elicited an audible gasp from the crowd. Even though she knew the number of words she can write in a day, she didn't know the exact number of books she'd written in her career. She thought she'd got about thirty-five books "out there, somewhere." She'd have forty soon.

In contemporary journalism about romance, it is common to lead a story by saying that it's a billion-dollar industry, the biggest single sector of book publishing, and that, according to the RWA, 3,000 romance novels are published a year, read by about 75 million readers. It is also common to pose the question: Why is it so popular? It is less common, though, to arrive at an answer that would do justice to the lives of a quarter of the population of the United States, or roughly half the population of women.

For the record, it's worth noting that these numbers are conservative estimates. They don't include library books or second-hand uses. They don't include the super-popular category of stand-alone downloadable short stories, which are a big market on digital platforms. Because so much of romance, including some of the biggest authors, is self-published, or, as they call it, indie, industry sales figures are understated. Because it is bigger than publishing's second-place category, religion, romance can be said to be bigger than Jesus. But even this kind of comparison hides as much as it reveals, because the two genres intersect: romance itself includes vast categories of religious or religious-lite novels.

On an average business day, a romance is published more than once an hour—more often than most newspapers update their stories online. The modern history of romance was linked with the magazine and newspaper form, and, I suspect, in its haste to publish and its eagerness to speak to what is happening right now, its heart is still there, mixed up directly in the business of everyday lives.

While journalists love to ask, *Why is romance so popular?* they rarely pose the more probing question: Why does romance's popularity constantly bother outsiders like themselves? What does it mean that a romance is born every few minutes in America, and almost as often, its readers are called upon to apologize for it? Those who dislike *The Da Vinci Code* or the latest Stephen King book tend to ignore it. But *Twilight,* and then *Fifty Shades of Grey,* which began as one reader's fan-fiction rendering of *Twilight,* sent people into what can best be described as panic mode. Deep was the level of condescension and loathing for *Twilight.* There were even anti-Mormon conspiracy theories surrounding its author. The charges against it sounded like those once leveled against the earliest novels, from the 1700s, written by women for other women, and for girls, that most feared demographic, and which were considered literally dangerous. Almost everyone I meet today, women in their twenties and thirties, who were teen megafans of *Twilight,* tend to speak of it with some embarrassment, and disavowal.

With *Fifty Shades,* this panic went into a second spasm, enough to generate subspecialties of academic research. One scholar spent an entire article documenting a distinct species of *Fifty Shades* critic: those who admitted, in their reviews, that they hadn't read the book. To repeat: there were enough reviewers whose refusal to *read a book* did not stop them from commenting, in print, at length, on this book, and in the harshest possible terms, that this type of review became a noteworthy genre of contemporary criticism.

There were vague, unsubstantiated charges that *Fifty Shades* would cause women to stay in abusive relationships. There were media reports that suggested that our culture was absorbing a wave of bodily injuries as readers tried to copy BDSM acts they'd read about in the story (which, as one Erotica author told me, would be "an argument for *more,* and better, BDSM lit, not less"). An article in *Harper's,* affecting a Joan Didion-in-the-'60s air of menaced paranoia, linked it to a real-life kidnapping. Any useful social or literary discussion of this book was quickly swallowed up in column after column of over-the-top denunciations, dark fantasies, and simple panic-mongering. And, apparently, also by scores of critics who performatively announced their refusal to read the book they were reviewing. That old canard—that romance books bring literal harm and ruin to readers—was alive and well in 2011. Apparently, women simply cannot be trusted around novels.

I was deeply curious about the power of books, to attract and to repel. Whatever its meaning, this widespread love-hatred of romance suggested to me that this form was alive.

This, to me, is why romance is America's national literature: not because it is universally read or admired but because it is universally obsessed over. That unresolved attitude toward pop romance—polarized, not incidentally, along gender lines—makes it one of our most important forms. It is our literature for the thorny and perennially troubling relationship we all—outsiders and fans—have with it, for what its stories reveal about us, and what we reveal about ourselves when we talk about it. To me, romance seemed to be a place where something big and important was still being decided. That's certainly what drew me to it. In a conversation with a romance editor, I once used the phrase "the role of romance within publishing," and she immediately stopped me, for a correction. "We *are* publishing," she said. She was talking about sales of romance books alone. But it's not just the genre's book sales. Few appreciate the degree to which romance readers form the core audience of other genres. Romance's readers, not just its authors, are among the most hardworking labor forces in literature.

Authors in those other genres know all about it. They see who shows up to events and who gives them boosts on social networks. Not that they want to admit it. I met a bestselling mystery author whose fan base consists of a significant population of romance readers (*"Shhhh,"* he told me, "don't tell anyone"). As a result, he has, he told me, "worked in some more romance plots, occasionally, over the years, where possible." Again, he added, *"Shhhh."*

Though it is remarkable that romance readers find time away from massively reading romance to also massively read other genres, there's an even more telling implication: while romance readers read other genres, non-romance readers do not read romance. The love is not reciprocated. On the contrary, if something is tagged "romance," many people will run the other way. This is another instance of a familiar cultural bias: in our stories, women (and members of any marginalized group) are constantly expected to identify with straight white male protagonists, but never the other way around. It is a training we all receive from a very young age in our culture.

It is also a familiar gender dynamic: women do more labor and receive less in exchange. In this case, as readers, they are called upon to sustain an entire genre of their own—which they have made into the single most popular on earth—and, in their spare time, they also help out other, male-dominated genres like mystery and religion. And what do they get in return?

Very little of that conflict is, however, apparent at the New Orleans Marriott during RT. Romance's overworked readers are too busy looking for the latest books and new authors. Many are looking to become authors themselves. Because romance is still a freewheeling world, a kind of literary Wild West, where indie publishing is growing and successfully competing with older gatekeepers, there's a conference room set aside at RT where conventioneers who have an idea for a book, or, better yet, a manuscript in hand, can pitch directly to the major publishers. I met women from all over the country, of all ages and from all walks of life, who didn't have any connections with editors in Manhattan, but who showed up in New Orleans that week— many of them staying two or more to a hotel room, to save money—hoping to get closer to becoming published authors.

There are moments at RT that feel and even look a bit like that scene in Kafka's unfinished novel, *Amerika,* in which Karl lands in an enormous theater that stretches "almost limitlessly" across the Oklahoma plains. Back in New York, he'd come across an advertisement that read: "Anyone thinking of the future, your place is with us! All welcome! Anyone who wants to be an artist, step forward! We are the theater that has a place for everyone!" Romance was exactly that: a theater that has a place for everyone. Everyone was invited to be an artist. All welcome!

Because Kafka didn't finish that novel, and our version of it ends in this theater, it could be described as the only story he wrote with a happy ending. But, more likely, given that it was Kafka, even this democratic utopia in the middle of America wasn't going to end happily. Similarly, Romancelandia had its dark corners. This I discovered at the "Signing Scams" panel.

Author signing scams involve someone who pretends to be organizing a big conference—the kind of mini-RTs that happen almost every weekend in hotels and conference centers all over America. This supposed organizer asks for some investments, and some deposits, then disappears without a trace. These scammers often pressure authors to sign up early, and then use these commitments to legitimize the scam to potential investors.

There was one such "publisher" who notoriously changed its name every year. One of the panelists told us, "Stay away from Love Den. *Bad news.*"

There was talk about one notorious thief, who went by the name Madeleine and presented herself as the owner of a successful pudding enterprise. "Maybe she was," mused the panelist. But Madeleine was no romance conference organizer. After this professed pudding-seller skipped out on a signing event she'd supposedly organized at a local hotel, she ran off, "to the Carolinas somewhere, I think." Pudding-monger Madeleine was never heard from again. Her co-organizers, who were legitimate romance people, were left to swallow the deposits and the contracts they'd made. They also looked foolish to their romance colleagues.

Some scammers, it turns out, may not be quite criminal but are "just people who got in over their heads." As romance continues to grow and prosper, so has its allure to fraudsters.

I happened to be sitting next to Nellie at this session. She rarely attended RT panels (unless she was presenting), as she was both too cool for it, and also busy with meetings, and, in any case, already completely in the know about everything. But the "Signing Scams" session had apparently caught her eye. When one of the panelists said, "Nobody thinks they're going to get scammed, but it happens all the time," Nellie leaned toward me and whispered, "Dude, you are so gonna get robbed, and, like, so hard."

Because I had too much riding on it, my optimism wouldn't be easily quashed. In that one way, at least, I was typical of an aspiring romancer. RT is how, in an earlier time in my career, I'd imagined the writing life. Even with its dark spots, it seemed mostly upbeat, hopeful, even joyous. The authors there didn't seem bitter—or, rather, they didn't let their bitterness define them. You can't, when you're writing romance. It would be a category error, because romance shares the essence of the comic genre: it is defined by its commitment to a happy conclusion. People who are drawn to romance, therefore, tend to be hopeful, and not because they are naïfs. On the contrary, they've seen some tough things—many romance authors launch their careers in midlife—and they have chosen to believe in something better.

At that RT in New Orleans, Nellie told me there were two kinds of people who became romance professionals. The first were lifelong readers of romance, devoted fans of the form. And the second were people who just loved publishing at its most energetic.

As a depressed person who is an optimist at heart, I wanted to share in this faith. Once, when I mentioned to a romance acquaintance of mine that some literary fiction writers I knew were doing a panel discussion on the age-old subject of "Is the novel in decline?" this person, who works in the romance industry, was perplexed by the premise. In genuine confusion, she said to me, "What? You mean because shorts and novellas have gotten so hot?"

This is part of what I immediately loved about romance

people. They didn't get the memo that the novel is in its death throes and that its readership has dwindled to, as Philip Roth predicted, "a small group of people. Maybe more people than now read Latin poetry, but somewhere in that range." Romance does not have that problem.

But it has other problems. It is beset by all kinds of economic and social turmoil. It took the RWA almost *four decades* to award a single RITA to a black author—a mind-bendingly damning fact about a publishing sector in which authors like Beverly Jenkins and Brenda Jackson have long been bestsellers. And even this change happened, in 2019, only after new regulations were rushed into effect following an insurgency of RWA members.

That particular conflict had escalated considerably when South African romancer Cherry Adair, freshly announced as the recipient of the RWA's Lifetime Achievement Award, addressed the #RitasSoWhite controversy by tweeting, "I agree 100% that this must change, but can't we wait five minutes for the finalists to enjoy their day?" or, as a blog post from *Black Chick Lit* put it: "Asking us all to wait to deal with racism so the finalists of this crooked contest can enjoy their day."

It got worse. Adair doubled down on her views. She continued to make revealingly bad decisions, like blocking not just her critics but also random writers of color who'd said not a word on the topic, much less against her, including some writers who were avowed fans. As pressure grew, especially on the RWA from its own members, so did the possibility of a real boycott of the event and of the organization generally. Adair eventually issued an apology and relinquished the award, which went without a recipient. And, even after all of that, the conflict over structural racism in the RWA hadn't yet begun.

At roughly the same time as the RITA controversy, another storm hit Romancelandia. An author named Faleena Hopkins somehow managed to officially trademark the word "cocky." Her registered trademark related not just to the word's design, as a logo, but to *any* use of the common English word "cocky" in any book series title. Cocky, it should be noted, had become something of a romance subgenre all its own. And Hopkins was something of a leader in the field, with her wildly successful Cocker Brothers of Atlanta series, and its twenty-plus installments (with titles like *Cocky Roomie, Cocky Cowboy, Cocky Genius, Cocky Senator*). For Hopkins, and for all authors of the Cocky subgenre, placing the word in the title makes it far more findable for readers, especially on digital platforms. Her trademark had an immediate monopolizing effect. It also spelled the start of a wider trademark war. Another romance author was already putting in the paperwork to obtain the trademark on the word "forever."

Only in the enterprising world of romance could a word that is traced to late-medieval English somehow become the exclusive property of a random white lady who lives in L.A., a self-described "novelist, actress, and filmmaker" who projected a sunny personality on her blog while dispatching lawyers to threaten other authors.

Once these threats went viral, Cockygate, as it would come to be known, escalated into a high-stakes legal war, fought in courts, on social media, and on the floor of the marketplace. For months Amazon, that overlord of contemporary bookselling, made the decision, per their cautious legal team, to pull *all* titles with the word "cocky" in them, even if they predated the new trademark—except for those by Faleena Hopkins. The devastating impact on her competitors in the Cocky subgenre was thus assured. This went on for months, until finally, and with the help of some RWA lawyers, a measure of temporary sanity was restored. Even though a settlement was reached in this case, it is only the beginning of a wider battle. Aggressive business interests, hungry for niche but lucrative monopolies, are watching closely. The radically democratic potential of romance is also a deep mine for the greedy.

I have never subscribed to the notion that romance is popular because of an easy-bake formula. But some hellish version of this idea is creeping into reality, thanks to scammers, and to Amazon. Some people, posing as romance authors, began manufacturing thousands of pages of cobbled-together texts, including openly plagiarized documents, into "books" that "readers," who were actually programmed bots, would then "read" in preposterously fast and numerous repetitions. It thus became possible to game the bestseller lists of Amazon's lucrative Kindle Unlimited (KU) program. Having thus climbed onto the bestseller lists, the bot developers managed to grab the spoils—some were making up to $50,000 a month—while taking up space and proceeds that belonged to others, i.e., to actual authors. For a matter of months, one of the most popular indie romance markets was barely distinguishable from a racket.

Quaint are the days when people hated Stephenie Meyer for her *Twilight* series: she was at least an actual author who wrote actual books for other actual human beings.

In short, romance has all kind of conflicts, but nobody believes that its problems are caused by the demise of the novel. On the contrary, the novel is doing perhaps too well. This overabundance of energy seemed, to me, like a good problem.

If there was any ambiguity about the political potential of tens of millions of women networking, organizing, crafting their own narratives, and leading an industry, the rhetoric at their gatherings left little doubt. At the 2019 RITA Awards ceremony, which came in the wake of that (first) political battle within the RWA over entrenched racism, one speaker after another pronounced the HEA as a call to arms. "Everyone deserves a happily ever after. *Everyone*" was said over and over again that night from the dais, to wild cheers. For its readers, the HEA is a standard of radical inclusivity. It is as simple and militant as women demanding their human right to pursue happiness. The phrase used in the RWA's official definition of the genre is "emotional justice." It was this principle, put into effect by its own members, that would eventually turn the RWA itself inside out. Despite Tolstoy's claim that happiness is so common that it is banal, the readers of romance, who are the democratic plurality of readers, know better. They know that happiness is painfully rare, and precious, and a story worthy of telling and retelling.

For me, the main draw to romance was just that: the stories themselves, about love and about emotional connections between people, stories that deal with these subjects in their full messiness but also end well. As a recent divorcé, I needed to go back to the drawing board, relationship-wise. If I was serious about making progress, I had best be intentional about it, and listen better. And, as a writer, this meant that it would be something I would explore through writing. I wanted to write in a way that was more vulnerable, a mode I was terrified to consider, for all the typically straight cis-male reasons. Romance seemed like a place to learn about love. And the fact that romance terrified the public, in my mind, was a good sign, because I myself was somewhat terrified about love. I had boarded my plane to New Orleans, RT-bound, with high hopes.

"We're basically the witches of the publishing world," one romance editor had said to me in New Orleans. "That's why you joined us, isn't it?"

It hadn't occurred to me that becoming a romance author was even an option until about a year earlier, at a bar in the Salt Lake City airport. I'd struck up a conversation with a very drunk older woman, a retired attorney from Austin, who had taken a liking to me. I knew that she'd taken a liking to me because she repeatedly said "I *like* you," forgetting each time, in her affably soused state, that she had just said so seconds earlier.

Her affection mostly took the form of pity. She was worried about me, she said, about my ability to make it as a writer. "You're not gettin' younger," she slurred. "Whaddya gonna do when you can't get by on your looks?" She reached into her purse and pulled out a book, with a shiny cover that depicted a woman's fingertips tantalizingly untying a corset. The title of the book was *Seduction of a Proper Gentleman.* It was indeed a proper romance, this one, with a cover of the type I would later learn was "all about the dress."

"Write one of *these*," she said. "*That's* how you make money as a writer."

When I rehearsed the problems I would likely encounter writing romance, the drunk woman cut me off.

"You're just like my son," she said. "Just do it, okay? For your mom."

As I dashed to my gate, I made a quick stop at the airport bookstore and grabbed a romance. By the time my plane landed in Boston, I had almost finished reading *Merry Christmas, Cowboy* by Janet Dailey. I had to admit I was intrigued. Could I really write one of these? Why not? It was a fun book, this *Merry Christmas, Cowboy.* I was curious to see where the cowboy would be, come Easter. Maybe the drunk woman at the airport bar was right. Though I knew that writing is almost never the fiscally responsible thing to do, it seemed like a particularly life-affirming way to be fiscally irresponsible.

Later I would meet a very sober person at a party who expressed disdain for romance. Someone had told her that I was interested in it, and that I'd even begun writing some of my own. She gave me a look—a narrow-eyed appraisal. In case I didn't get the message, she also said it directly. She'd never read one, she said. And, to be clearer yet, she added that she wouldn't. In her words, "I wouldn't be caught dead reading one of *those* books."

She seemed an intelligent, good-humored, and empathetic

person who would be genuinely aghast to learn that an opinion she openly espouses might be ignorant, and maybe even a bit bigoted. She was, I would learn, an attorney, a member of the ACLU. She had a recurring donation to public radio because she firmly believed in evidence-based conclusions, "especially these days." But when it came to the subject of America's most loved books, she felt no need to have read one, nor even to hold that reading a romance is, in principle, a prerequisite for an evidence-based conclusion. This one was self-evident. These stories are, she said, "bad for your health."

"They call them 'trashy novels' for a reason," she added.

She didn't say this in the spirit of provocation but rather with the full expectation that everyone within earshot obviously agreed with this truth, universally acknowledged.

She might have also said they were politically regressive, that they're artifacts of rape culture, and a variety of other arguments that have been made against romance, especially in the past. In my opinion, those are the more interesting critiques. Hers was simply the oldest take: trashy novels are trash (and so are the people who read them). That was the view of Nathaniel Hawthorne, who used the word "trash" as early as 1855, in reference to the novels written by the "damned mob of scribbling women," which far outsold his own.

I wasn't in the mood to argue with the woman at the party. Like many a romance sympathizer, I often find myself in a defensive posture. It gets old. I shrugged at the woman's comment. But then something strange happened. Strange, not because it was uncommon—strange because it happened with remarkable regularity, almost a kind of inevitability. I asked the woman whether she'd ever read a romance when she was young. After thinking about it for a moment, she realized she had, and also that she'd completely forgotten about it. In excavating the memory she was, it seemed, experiencing a strange replay of some important moment in her life.

There was, she told me, a period in junior high when she hung out a lot with a certain friend—a dear friend she'd barely thought about in years. They used to creep into her friend's aunt's apartment and pilfer romances from the shelf, then run back to her house, close the bedroom door, and read the books together aloud, in a kind of stage whisper, giggling through the racy parts. And then they'd sneak the books back onto the aunt's shelf, sincerely fearing that they would get caught. It had been their secret, theirs alone, their bond.

"I guess that's kind of how we learned about sex," she told me, laughing at this sudden unexpected discovery. "Maybe this explains some things about me."

She seemed amused, disturbed, and somewhat embarrassed to discover, and in so public a way, that *those books* were important to her at a formative moment in her life. Her story is typical. I have heard it, with slight variations, dozens of times (it is the reason why I'd asked her the question). As an old friend of mine would later remind me, I myself had such a story, with slightly different details: in our case it was the friend's mother's romance novels, and they were stashed in her bedroom, and we *did* get caught. I'd also forgotten that I'd been a romance reader once. My romance quest as an adult, it turned out, was a rediscovery, an excavation of some lost part of myself.

———

Once I started paying attention, I began to see that romance lit was everywhere, hidden in the proverbial closets of our lives and our society. How was it possible that the most common books in our culture were also so concealed? I started by testing my theory that "romance is everywhere" by seeing how many romance novels I could read even if I didn't actually buy or check one out of the library. I would read only what came to hand in the natural order of city life: whatever was left around in cafés, on the curb, on the subway. This yielded at least a novel a week. Maybe more like 1.5 novels a week. I was never without one. And I read all of them.

But none of this meant that I actually could write one. I'd begun making a serious search for help, in the form of a romance writing group. I'd taken some suggestions from some RWA-affiliated people, but it seemed laughably premature to get involved with RWA. I wasn't ready. Then I got lucky. A writers' group came to me at my own laundromat.

In between my tossing a load into the dryer and returning to check on it, someone had posted a sign for a group that met nearby. They were romance writers who were "casual but serious" about their work. They were looking for another writer or two for their group. Even before I unloaded my laundry, I called the number. The woman who answered was half a block away, since she'd just posted the sign.

The group assembled in the back of a dive bar, like a gang of mafiosi plotting a heist. That first day there were six of us: five women—Aparna, Janice, Linda, Heather, Janna—and me. The group's organizers, Aparna and Janice—the latter had posted the notice—quickly revealed themselves to be a kind of odd couple. Aparna, the cool customer, and Janice, a self-identified "nervous Nellie." They were also probably about twenty years apart in age and in stylings—Aparna with tats and an asymmetric hairdo, dyed purple-pink tiger stripes, and Janice straight-edged, with a church-bake-sale vibe.

Aparna created such enormous quantities, and also unusual qualities, of vapor from her ever-present vape pipe that I must, in the name of honest reporting, dwell for a moment on a description. In her vaping she resembled some kind of urbane mastermind in a comic book, sitting back nonchalantly, draping herself in silky smoke. At times, the only element visible behind the vapor was a single purple-outlined eye. At times, she disappeared completely, with a sudden swooshing gesture, in an impressively giant puff, like a vampire making a dramatic exit. It's highly unlikely that the smoke itself was purple but, in my memory, that's how it appears.

During that first meeting, the stories and the conversation around the stories were lively and easy. But when the time came to discuss my first story, there was a palpable change in the air. People shifted in their seats and exchanged nervous glances.

Nobody dared say a word. There was actual throat clearing. I had the strong urge to gather my papers, bow, say "Ladies," and run out of the room. The only sound we could hear was Aparna inhaling a huge drag off her pipe. It was clear that the situation demanded leadership, and so we all waited for Aparna to open.

And then, from deep inside a fantastic swirl of endless, possibly purple, vapor, Aparna's voice spoke forth.

"I feel . . . like," Aparna said. "I feel like the hero of this story didn't have to be so . . . *decrepit*? Is that the right word?"

"*Yes,*" Janna interjected, "that's exactly the right word!"

"Like," Aparna continued, "I think I get *why* he's a werewolf? But why does he have to be a *dying* werewolf, you know? Like literally he dies. He can't *die.*"

It suddenly occurred to me that I'd have to make some changes in my next story, which was to feature a decrepit Viking.

Linda spoke up now. "Maybe he should be just horribly *injured.*"

There was a sudden surge of electricity in the bar. The overhead lights brightened horribly, and an AC unit whirred into overdrive. There was an overall sense that a powerful current was alive and coiling itself around us. I don't remember anything else from that meeting.

For the next one, I decided to pre-workshop my workshop story. To avoid a repeat of the massacre from the first meeting, I consulted an acquaintance who was steeped in the romance genres. I showed her three stories, in various states of disrepair, with a note asking her to flag "anything that's passable or salvageable or even remotely romance-worthy." I knew it would be a chore. We spoke by phone.

"You're a professional writer. Can I be honest?"

"Oh, God, okay."

"I've read your published stuff. I get that your stories are sometimes sort of . . . I don't know, pointless. But like intentionally. I don't mean pointless, I mean plotless. But anyway, they're definitely not boring even when they are basically pointless. I mean, plotless! They're *energetic*," she said suddenly, "and that's, I think, the most important to do in writing."

"Mm-hm," I said.

"But these romance stories are just not working. They don't have that energy in them."

"Hmm," I said.

"And here's the other problem, I think. They're not romance."

"I'm guessing you're talking about the Jerusalem story?" I said, shuffling papers to pull it out.

In that story, a Holy Land pilgrim from Kentucky becomes infatuated with her tour guide. At the Holy Sepulchre in Jerusalem, she realizes something important about love and herself. She sees a scene of pilgrims pressing their faces in frantic prayer against a stone slab, "like forlorn dogs sniffing at the sock of a beloved owner, after he has departed, leaving them abandoned—alone, together, forever." That was the last line of my romance story.

"Well, since you brought it up? Yeah, that one for sure," she said.

"What part didn't work?" I said. "The love story?"

"The *love* story?" she said. "No, it didn't work. I think you need to read way more romance."

"I am!"

"Okay, well. Let's put it this way: your HEA was not an HEA. Like, not even close."

I brightened up at this.

"Oh, I can totally see why you'd say that," I said, as though there'd been some kind of silly misunderstanding. "Maybe I wasn't clear. It's a happy ending because she *finally* realizes that she's totally alone. Like, epiphany-style? Or, actually, she realizes . . . not that she is alone in being alone, but that she's just like everyone else, who, when you boil it down, is also alone. So she feels this sense of *togetherness* . . . in the sudden awareness of being alone?"

I realized that I was sounding like a divorced guy.

"Anyway, it's just not a *romance* story," she said finally. "If you're asking me what I think, I wouldn't bring these to your group."

The only thing I'd written that was ready to go, romance-wise, was a story called "A Catered Affair" about an overworked, prickly veteran caterer who finds love with a guy who delivers smoked fishes, and who delivers other things, too. I had mixed feelings about it. But at least it stuck to the rules.

And what were those rules, exactly? I'd come across Pamela Regis's Eight Essential Elements of the Romance Novel. Regis is a literary scholar and historian who developed categories for analyzing existing texts. She didn't write how-to books. But I figured I might use her formulations to reverse-engineer some romance copy out of them. I printed out her Eight Essential Elements and posted it on my wall. They are:

1. Society Defined
2. The Meeting
3. The Barrier
4. The Attraction
5. The Declaration

6. The Point of Ritual Death
7. The Recognition
8. The Betrothal

For good measure, Regis identified three additional elements that are common but not essential to the form: 1) A Wedding, Fete, or Dance; 2) Scapegoat Exiled; 3) The Bad Punished.

This was, it seemed, a version of the reviled formula, so often cited by romance haters, as the thing that makes the genre so damnable. But to romance readers, this is where it gets interesting. In this way, they are like any kind of fan. What makes basketball interesting to its fans is that the rules and dimensions of the game are explicit and fixed: the basket is ten feet tall for everyone who steps onto the court, and the question is always, *What path will the ball travel to land into that hoop* this *time?* For that to have meaning, the ball, the court, and the hoop, and the rules guiding play, must be the same every time. To the non-fan, this all seems repetitious. But its devotees know, because they have the expert eyes to see, that those repetitions are essential because they create the conditions for greater and subtler forms of variety.

Romance readers give a lot of thought to genre. To them, the questions of form and genre aren't just marketing categories and demographic targets, they are about what matters most in a story. And, like fans, they process all of this information together, openly.

At RT I witnessed a panel wrap up its conversation by playing a call-and-response game with the audience. A panelist would throw out a single plot-twist scenario. After that, she shouted out a genre, and the crowd was invited to propose the next plot point, based on the genre. For the story scenario, she pulled a piece of paper out of a hat that read: *The head of the family has died.*

Now she turned to the crowd with a genre.

"Okay . . . ," she shouted. *"Mystery!"*

"Who murdered him!" someone shouted back immediately from the crowd.

"Good! Now . . . *Epic!"*

"How did this mess begin?" another voice said from the back of the room.

"Paranormal!"

"What does the dead person's house *look* like!"

". . . and, if *Paranormal Shapeshifter*? . . ."

"Who will take over the pack!"

"Historical!"

"Who is the legitimate heir!"

"Good! Okay. *Coming-of-Age Literary Fiction!"*

"So much painnn!" someone shouted. "SO MUCH suffering!"

Everyone in the room laughed.

I was enchanted by how fluent romance readers were in the language of genre. I wanted to see the world like that, too.

I wanted the rules. I needed the rules. It felt like a question of survival. Love and relationships were a crisis for me. I had a love story to figure out, the one central to my own life, and I was desperate to figure out how to construct it. Desperate even to learn how to ask the right questions: What must come next in the story? What were the options?

———

Only hours before I'd boarded the flight to New Orleans, I had found myself in a Boston-area courtroom for a divorce hearing. My short marriage—the final chapter of a long relationship—had crumbled over the last year and a half, and I suddenly found myself standing next to a woman I loved and knew so well, and who had been my closest friend since college, offering sworn testimony before a smirking magistrate.

The Honorable Judge A. had sauntered into the courtroom still chewing the last bite of his breakfast, wiping his mouth with his robe, and kidding around with his deputy. Even as we took our solemn oaths, the judge seemed to have some joke on his mind. Throughout the proceedings he struggled to suppress a major fit of the giggles.

The aura of sheer goofiness that surrounded the judge was not lost on my soon-to-be ex-wife. Without even looking at her, I knew that she was finding this display of judicial farce as darkly entertaining as I was. Even though we were breaking up and we rarely saw each other in those days, we could still communicate nonverbally. We had made an unstated pact to avoid making eye contact, lest our amusement shatter what remained of courtroom decorum, not to mention the very real gravity of the moment. But when the hearing was finally over, she and I walked out, closed the court door behind us, exchanged a look, and, for a moment, we both laughed.

Nothing that day could compare to the deep comedy that had been our first divorce proceeding, some weeks earlier, at the Orthodox Jewish Beth Din of Greater Boston, also known as the Rabbinical Court of Justice. This court, it turned out, was located in a converted dentist-office space off Boston Common, which gave me the chance to make good on a piece of wisdom. An editor at *Salon* magazine recently had asked me to contribute to a piece entitled "*Salon's* Guide to Writing a Memoir," where I would join a group of memoirists who were giving advice to aspiring memoirists. (Ta-Nehisi Coates had offered: "Don't lie. Seriously, don't fucking lie.") My advice, in addition to "Give therapy a shot," included these sage words: "If you get your wisdom teeth out, decline sedation anesthesia. I was wide awake when I had my wisdom teeth pulled and got to hear Cyndi Lauper's 'Girls Just Want to Have Fun' playing on the radio as the dentist undertook his ghastly labors. These are the cherished moments for the writer of narrative nonfiction." The *Salon* editor—who would herself go on to write a bestselling memoir, subtitled *Remembering the Things I Drank to Forget*—cut this piece of brash medical advice from the article, citing legal concerns. But now, at my Orthodox Jewish divorce hearing, a teeth pulling of its own, I had a chance to take my own advice, to "decline sedation anesthesia," as it were, and to face the dentist's office with eyes and ears wide open.

It was worse than gory. It was friendly. Or, in the gothic language of the divorced, "amicable." And we would immediately pay the price for it. As we sat in the waiting room of this dentist's office/Rabbinical Court of Justice, we couldn't help ourselves: we fell into a familiar intimacy and began to catch up by exchanging gossip and photos. A very young, very Orthodox woman, the only other person in the waiting room, seemed charmed by our conversation and, after a moment of unsubtle eavesdropping, leaned toward us and asked, with a youthful blush of expectation, if we were there to pick up a marriage license.

Soon enough, however, we were relieved of this unbearably sad form of awkwardness by a more urgent and alarming form of awkwardness. One of the three presiding rabbis, I learned, was a former teacher of mine, from my days at the local Orthodox Jewish high school. I was apprised of this fact a moment before the proceedings. The junior rabbi had tapped me on the shoulder and whispered, "Is it okay if Rabbi K. sits on your beis din?"

As it happened, Rabbi K., a brilliant scholar and a creative soul, was one of the few rabbis I had always admired. But when I looked up and saw him standing there, leaning very uncomfortably against the door, waving slowly at me, I did wonder if this might be a literal nightmare: the ridiculously implausible logic that would have a former high school teacher presiding over your divorce.

We pressed on with the hearing. Within seconds, the court's senior rabbi determined that I was indeed the son of a well-known Jewish educator in the Boston area.

"You're *Bernie's* son!" he said, throwing his hands up in the air, and looking around to his fellow rabbis for confirmation of just how amazing this was.

I tried to see it through his eyes. This was just a regular Monday for him. He was just trying to pass the time until lunch. As soon as we were done here, he'd retreat into the office kitchenette and treat himself to some babka. I'd already seen this babka—chocolate, obviously—messily cut with a plastic knife, and lined up on a foam plate, one for each member of the Rabbinical Court.

We played a short but intense game of Jewish Geography, an exercise that strongly resembled a tennis-ball machine firing out juicy, slow and steady shots for the rabbi to swat back over the net. Sometimes he needed to sprint to catch up, but most were clean hits for him.

You went to Maimonides School?—*whack!*

You must know Baruch Shapiro. You do?—*ding!*

Oh, you were in the same class?—*thwack!*

Soon we were talking Torah. Talmud. Medieval commentaries. When he seemed satisfied that I hadn't forgotten everything I'd been taught, we moved on. He asked me about my writing.

"Prison? Very *interesting,*" he said. "Did they have anyone on death row there?"

When I told him they did not, he seemed disappointed. He also seemed uninterested to learn that the woman sitting silently next to me was a chief resident at Mass General Hospital, and was unmoved by some other facts about her that could be topics of conversation.

Finally the elder rabbi just shook his head, looked us over, and said, "You both seem great—so *what's the problem?* I really don't understand. Maybe you can explain it to me? Nu, Avi, why are so many young people getting divorced these days?"

I hoped it was a rhetorical question. It was not.

"Any theories?" he continued. "I'd appreciate if someone could explain it to me."

I exchanged looks with my fellow sufferers. I could see that my former teacher, a sensitive soul, was sitting silently on this council, dying inside as he listened to his elder colleague chatting away. But as we sat at the head office of the patriarchy, most of my feeling was with my about-to-be ex, the only woman in this room of men, who was being almost completely ignored.

Because I knew her well, I guessed that she was shaking off their insulting treatment simply because it also offered her relief. The last thing she wanted to do was chat with these rabbis right now. She was fine letting me handle it. In fact, I think she was getting some perverse joy in watching me squirm before the old boys. Mostly, she was sad, as I was; we both looked reduced in the face.

A couple years earlier, when she was in her first year of medical school, she'd written a painfully beautiful poem about dissecting a cadaver in her anatomy class, an old man who had left this world with an enlarged heart. The poem was also about me, or, rather, about us, and about her fear, her projected grief, really, in imagining me suddenly gone from her life. Thinking back on it, I wondered if maybe the poem had been about her knowing, even back then, that it was already over between us.

The divorce happened in a room that would have been a surgical space back when the Rabbinical Court was a dentist's office. We did the ceremony, a kind of slapstick exercise that involved my walking out of the room, fully down the hall ("*all* the way down," the junior rabbi cautioned me), and then back, handing her the divorce document, the *get,* at which point she was instructed to walk around the room with it, as though trying on a new pair of shoes.

When we finally emerged from the Rabbinical Court, it was a bright and sunny day on Boston Common, and we decided to grab some food. We rarely talked anymore, but here we were, at lunchtime, and we'd just survived this thing together, so why not? As we ate, she turned to me and said, "Well, at least you can use this for a story, right?" She did a quick spot-on improvisation of the rabbis deliberating with each other.

The *get* was her request. She'd felt a bit guilty, dragging me back into this Orthodox world, knowing that it was difficult for me. She'd always had my back like that. And I knew it was important to her to have this document, so we'd soldiered through it.

But it was the kindness in her statement that had gotten me. She'd always been a major supporter of my aspirations. As a sometimes writer herself, a satirist, she knew good material when she saw it. For a moment, I was touched by her encouragement. Then came the pang of heartbreak, for which I would have to breathe deeply, so that it would not feel shattering.

Immediately we caught ourselves. The dark shadow passed between us. Our ability to share even the bitter moment of divorce *together*—just as we'd shared so many others—only made the moment more affecting, more untenable. Our marriage hadn't fallen apart because we'd lost our rapport. We'd met when she was nineteen and I was twenty-one years old. Laughter was, in fact, our earliest and most lasting connection. For many years, that bond had been enough. But now, it wasn't.

On my way to the divorce court, I'd caught my reflection in a shop's plate-glass window, and spotted, for the millionth time, the funny way I walk: a bit bowlegged and with a short strut, like a small overbred dog who thinks he's a big dog. It was my ex who first pointed this out to me. She used to tease me about my gait and could do a perfect impression of it. That's how it is with people who love you. They show you how to see yourself, how to know yourself, how to appreciate yourself. In happier days, she had said that it gave her joy to see that silly little march coming toward her from all the way up the street, even before she could see my face. And yet it hadn't been enough. Whenever people spoke of the formula in romance stories—the thing that made lasting love plausible to so many millions of people—all I could think was, *I need to know what that formula is.* I needed to try something new.

Picking a genre mattered because it would help determine nothing less than what kind of life I would try to live, what kind of ending I imagined for my life story. Was it the So Much Suffering of Coming-of-Age Literary Fiction, or was it something else? Could it be romance? Could that be a story I truly believed in? For my entire life, in my personal life and education, I have been taught that the HEA is bullshit—or worse, some kind of delusion—and some part of me will always remain skeptical. But I also had come to realize that this skepticism had become a kind of convenience, a way of never taking love or happiness seriously. And not taking love or happiness seriously is an ethical failure: it makes one a vampiric presence in the lives of others.

At RT, subgenres appeared on tags everywhere: on lanyards, and at sales tables, at virtually every session at the conference, every expert panel. Your subgenre was a kind of identity marker in the community. And, to its writers, it mattered most because it was the critical first step in helping clarify the next plot point, to help identify the big question that would move the story forward. And I really wanted to move my story forward.

I woke up early on the second morning of RT New Orleans to prepare for my first test as a romance author, even though, at that point, I'd written roughly no publishable romance. An event dubbed "Pitch-a-Palooza" gave aspiring authors a chance to talk business with industry people. Though it filled me with intense dread, I wasn't going to squander the opportunity to walk around a hotel ballroom full of publishers and agents sitting at tables, who were fielding book proposals. Each pitch could be no more than three minutes—how bad could that be?

As I waited in the giant snaking line outside the hotel ballroom, listening to people practice their proposals for *The Next Fifty Shades,* I got a text message. It was from Emma, a recent ex. When we'd first met, we'd been in similar circumstances: married for a short time to someone whom we'd been with for many years, and now separated. Though we lived thousands of miles apart, we'd found ways to end up in various random cities for trysts. Part of the attraction for me had been that safe distance between us.

That was my instinct at this moment in my life. After my separation, I'd gone out and found myself possibly the tiniest bedroom on the eastern seaboard. And, in this tiny room, the tiniest bed I'd ever seen for an adult who wasn't in a coffin. I had literally no space for anyone in my life. I barely had room for my own feet.

I found myself suddenly noticing men all over town who gave me pause. The sweet man who wore a bicycle helmet with bumper stickers on it, at all times, even when he wasn't on his bicycle. He sat on benches feeling so desperate for human connection that he ended up lecturing children about where rain comes from until their mothers noticed and herded them away. Was that how things go? First the tiny bed, then the permanent bicycle helmet with bumper stickers?

Having learned that a romance proposal involves a series, not just a single book, I'd hatched an idea. From my recent work, I happened to know a bit about Mormon history. A romance series, in the popular Historical genre, thus presented itself: the tangled web of a polygamous Mormon family. Each book in the series would center on the love plot of a different "sister wife." I'd already decided which traits to explore for each. There would be Alice's terrifying inability to refrain from telling the whole truth; Emmeline's capacity for getting herself into absurd situations, matched only by her talent for masterfully narrating the story about it later; and secretive Anna, with her big, lustrous hair and a mysterious inner world that she expressed through mesmerizing drawings.

But I kept it simple. I explained that the series would be similar to the popular Amish Romance subgenre, but unlike those books, my books would be more frankly erotic. The "sister-wife" plot, which had already proved popular for TV, was destined to be a hit with romance readers. Thus went my pitch.

The idea went over better than I had expected. After being politely passed over by Penguin Random House, told that the idea was "a bit too niche," I got very positive reactions from many of romance's other heavy hitters: Avon, Kensington, Harlequin, Grand Central, and the smuttier and since defunct Ellora's Cave.

The Ellora's Cave editor cautioned me about the polygamy premise. "That's *your* fantasy," she said to me, with a knowing smile, "not ours." But she added that this could be managed with the right POV, and a few deft plot turns. (Later, my shrink would ask me, with a raised eyebrow, "Why *did* you propose a series about polygamy?" and didn't buy my reply that it simply made for good serial storytelling.)

A few editors at "Pitch-a-Palooza" wrote their private office extensions on their cards, signaling genuine interest. The most enthusiastic responses I got were from editors at two imprints at Harlequin, one of whom was so keen that she asked to see five chapters of the work in progress that afternoon, if possible.

"I'm serious," she'd said, handing me her card. "Send me those chapters!"

I didn't have even one chapter to give her. Even if I had, I doubt I would have felt confident about it. By the end of the first half of the convention, I was falling into a deeper funk. I skipped a morning of the convention and sat in bed, absently reading from the Book of Mormon, conveniently placed in all Marriott hotel end-table drawers. I stared out my window list-lessly, watching the barges drift by on the big muddy river, which seemed like the kind of thing a divorced person should do.

My body did eventually leave my room, and attend a few pan-els, including an intriguing one about the rising subgenre of Amish Romance ("it's a response to *Fifty Shades*," one panelist conjectured), but I was feeling almost too depressed to bend my knees, much less to walk. I moped about the lobby of the Marriott, where I stuck out, if not exactly like a sore thumb, like a sadly overdressed and underfed thumb. In the lobby mirrors I observed myself, surrounded by smiling women wearing Texas-shaped brooches, exchanging loud reunion greetings with friends, as giant posters of half-naked hunks loomed behind them.

After I got my boxed lunch, I quickly shuffled to the elevator, looking down at the floor the whole way. In a different giant mirror I watched myself, clutching a tuna sandwich, with a far-away look on my face, waiting for the elevator to close. And when it did, I was replaced by the poster on the elevator doors: an image of literally monstrous male abdominal muscles that likely belonged to a werewolf.

That evening, as it got dark, I remained in my room, incapacitated, trying to stay as quiet as humanly possible. My mood had deepened considerably, but some of my convention friends were urging me to come out. It was time for the ball.

I was sitting on an immaculately white bed, propped up by four gigantic, immaculately white hotel pillows, holding my breath. The TV was off and so were the lights. Outside, the sun had set and it was rapidly darkening. I was ignoring the knocking on my door by a very nice but also insistent woman from Wisconsin. All day she had been trying to persuade me to attend the night's Saints & Sinners Party in the hotel's Grand Ballroom. I knew that she was dressed as a sinner because hours earlier she had described the whole glittery, strategically torn ensemble to me. Now that she was knocking on my door and calling my name, I was feeling particularly low. It was rude and cowardly to ignore her. But I was in no mood to be social. So I sat on the bed and barely breathed until she left. I would see people tomorrow, in the light of day. Tonight I would just sit on ice.

It had been untold number of hours now. Down at RT, the Saints & Sinners Party was either still happening in the Grand Ballroom or it was long over. I searched for my legal pad, hidden somewhere toward the endless, blindingly white horizon of the massive hotel bed. When I finally found it, I got to work on the first installment of my Mormon sister-wife romance series. I would do some plotting. My pen slid all the way to the bottom of the page, where I wrote: *The HEA*. I drew a target around it. At least I knew what I was aiming at. I might not be one of the romance pros on the "Writing Quickly" panel who can write ten thousand words a second with my toes, while lying in traction. But I wasn't going down without a fight.

"Look at us up here," one of those "Writing Quickly" authors had said, "a panel of Scheherazades."

To which her co-panelist, who'd self-described as "trading cluster migraines for some success in publishing," replied, "Yeah, in my case, Scheherazade in dirty sweats on Facebook."

Scheherazade, the narrator of *One Thousand and One Nights,* sometimes known as *The Arabian Nights,* saves herself from execution, for nearly three years, by inventing nightly stories for the benefit of her one-person audience, a murderous king. She must constantly outdo herself, constantly up the ante, story-wise—or else.

As a child, I loved the stories of Aladdin and Ali Baba, but, as a grown-up, and especially once I worked as a writer, I came to realize that the true hero of that book is its narrator. Her plight, the story of her journey of survival, is the meta-story of *Nights*. Scheherazade is the model of the audience-aware storyteller, the patron goddess of all writing, and especially of popular literature. The story of Scheherazade gets at how the storyteller wields immense power, yet, at the same time, is radically vulnerable to the whims of her audience. Her power, in fact, is tied to those whims, to the way she bravely and skillfully harnesses them to propel her stories.

After that "Writing Quickly" panel, I did a Google search of Scheherazade, and one of the top hits was "Is the *Arabian Nights* a true story?" What I discovered at RT is that it absolutely is a true story. Scheherazade, she who speaks in many voices, and tells her stories at the edge of the sword of her listener, walked the halls of the New Orleans Marriott that week.

Like a romance author, Scheherazade tells stories in a range of genres; the guiding principle is Whatever Works, whatever mesmerizes the listener at that moment. Romance authors are the least romantic creatives out there. They are pragmatists through and through. Pop romance writers, like Scheherazade, might spin tales of romance, but they thrive on a shrewd, worldly grasp of power relationships.

It's no accident that the narrator of *Nights* is a woman. Her predicament speaks to the inherent trap of being a woman in a society that makes impossible demands of women: to be everything at once, or else to be nothing at all. It is a kind of storytelling that begins from the distinctly unprivileged position of having your head on the chopping block. Romance, because it is audience-centered, is in some ways similar to a service industry, and, like most service industries, it is women who make up most of the workforce. Like Scheherazade, a romance author might survive, but it will be always against the odds. No wonder the romance authors on the "Writing Quickly" panel identified with her, as they described their literary stress injuries. Even Scheherazade, after a thousand nights, finally called it off.

And when she did, she achieved something of an HEA. The frame story of *A Thousand and One Nights* ends on what could be seen as a hopeful note. On her thousandth-and-first night, Scheherazade and the king make peace, and they are betrothed. *Nights,* it turns out, is a romance. But this HEA is more of a cease-fire than a truly happy reconciliation. Perhaps the HEA of *Nights* is really about something else. At the end of the tale, Scheherazade has achieved a kind of undeniable power, a legendary status as a storyteller. She becomes, in effect, a famous author. In contemporary romance-publishing terms, she's left with a massive backlist of stories—which, as I learned at RT, is the key for the enterprising indie romance author—and in a dizzying array of subgenres. She is the kind of storyteller who has more stories than she could remember. What she remembers most about them: each one was absolutely necessary.

But if Scheherazade is a myth of the individual successful romance author, the triumph of the female storyteller in a cutthroat male-dominated world, what about all the women who aren't as successful? Even in *Nights,* we get a glimpse of that dark equation: many entered the king's chamber, and all, until Scheherazade, were put to death.

As I descended an escalator at RT, the giant head of Sylvia

Day, followed by a black choker, suddenly rose in front of me like a planet.

"God, that's creepy," said a fellow RT-goer, as we gazed at the banner. "It's like one of those dictators or something."

"Not a Sylvia fan?" I asked, as we got off the escalator.

"Nah," she said. But then added: "Well, in a way, I am. I mean, I'm basically trying to *be* her." This woman was headed to a panel called "So You're Published—Now What?"

Because RT brought the many types of romancers together under a single roof, it was also one of the few places where you could watch the community's dramas unfold in real-time. All around the conference there were small moments of tension along lines of race, class, sexual orientation, and age. Sometimes all at once. I was standing right next to a younger black woman, whose nametag identified her as the author of contemporary LGBT romances, when she accidentally walked into a panel on Regency romances, Historicals, the old-guard genre of romance. This author quickly surveyed the huge room of older white women, did a double take at her program, and said to herself, but audibly, "Um, *no,*" immediately did an about-face, and exited.

When I'd caught up with her later and asked her about it, she laughed. "Oh, you saw that? Well . . . right. Not my scene." I asked her to elaborate. "Oh, I got nothing against them," she said. "I like some of those books. Just as long as there's plenty of room for my stuff, too, I'm fine. And, hey, if they want to buy my books, that's even better."

With my Mormon sister-wives Historical series now in progress, I found that I was toeing some genre lines, and could use some guidance. When I walked into a session called "Winning at Cross-Genre," which was half full, I caught the conclusion of a story that one of the panelists was telling. I entered just as she was saying "... and it ended up being a shapeshifter story with a Husky!" Everyone in the audience replied, *"Awwww."*

As usual, there were many solid, numerical pieces of advice. "Romance readers will read seven books a week," a panelist noted. "Mystery readers won't." This is good to know if you're trying to appeal to both readerships. "It's easier to get Historical readers to migrate to other genres," we were told. "But it's very hard to get people to Historicals."

After the panel I spoke with a young romancer, who publishes under the name Mimi Milan, a well-regarded author. She was attending her first RT, along with her five-year-old daughter.

"I may need a new name," she told me, as people were clearing out. "But I'm trying to figure that out."

I immediately grasped why she seemed so glum about that. Mimi Milan had a nice thing going. Readers know and trust that name. I'd often heard authors say that readers must *trust* them. Readers, too, often used that word. The Mimi Milan name was trusted. She'd published a series of well-received books in the Inspirational (read: Christian) genre and in Sweet Romance, a genre that doesn't allow explicit sex or dark plot elements in it. Amish Romance, too, was of this genre. If Amish tended to flash a bonnet on the cover, Sweet Romance often featured a puppy. But now Mimi Milan was thinking of going edgier, sexier, and possibly more queer. Her new tagline, featured on her website at the time, was "Sugar and Spice and *Everything.*"

This is not a decision to be taken lightly. How does an indie author like her, who's struggled and succeeded to cultivate a readership, gained that precious trust, and managed to secure a loyal following especially among her target demo of Latina readers, make this transition without losing those readers? This was the question that had brought her to the "Winning at Cross-Genre" session. One of the authors had spoken to her dilemma: "If you do Inspirational and Erotic, use different names. If you write whips-n-chains and YA, use different names! Kids don't care, obviously, but parents do."

A name change was the obvious choice. I'd met authors who used a dozen names, at various points in their career. Some couldn't remember all of them. When one author I spoke to had trouble tallying her former names, she said to me, "This is kind of like counting up your sex partners. It's not always fun." Another called some of her old names "my bastard children."

Milan was also aware that a new name meant no existing backlist. She'd have to work double and triple time to start pumping out new novels and novellas and holiday-hooked stand-alone stories to build up that list. This new author brand would have zero followers. So a name change was one way forward, but it was a setback to be avoided, if possible.

There was another way, she told me. Maybe she could write herself out of this problem. Maybe she could make the crossing of genres, from innocence to experience, into the narrative itself, and spin this journey into the Mimi Milan heroes' and heroines' own quests. She'd noticed that her core group of religious readers seemed ready to follow her into this new territory. ("They sit in church and talk about *Fifty Shades,*" Milan told me. "*Inside* the church.") As her young daughter rolled around impatiently over the conference-room seats next to her, Milan detailed the pros and cons. But she was confident she could make the move from Inspirational to "Sugar and Spice and *Everything*," if she was clever about it.

"I know I can do it," she told me, and paused. "But the readers will *definitely* let me know."

In the weeks before New Orleans, I visited the RT company office in downtown Brooklyn. I'd met up with Carol Stacy, a romance veteran, and, at the time, publisher of *RT Book Reviews*.

When I'd referred to the upcoming gathering as being "two months from now," I was immediately corrected by another RT staffer, the woman in charge of conference logistics, Tere Michaels, who's also a romance author. ("Actually," Michaels had said to me, "it's seven weeks away. And counting.") Michaels was on a war footing. The convention was a year-round, full-time job.

The RT offices had giant picture windows that caught full sunlight. It was one of the mellower and cheerier New York media offices I'd been in. The place was typical NY industrial low-key chic, high ceilings, walls painted white, creaky hardwood floors, four desks, an office or two, and a conference room with stiff IKEA couches and coffee tables. I sat there with Tere Michaels and Carol Stacy, who's been with RT since the beginning and has pretty much seen it all in the romance world. In the old days, the RT convention was smaller, a bit more insular, and by all accounts more wild. When I asked Carol Stacy about those old gatherings, she just said, "Oh, yeah, there're some stories there, lemme tell you." One year they decided to organize a cross-country train ride, and picked up people as they made their way across America to the convention. "We called it the Love Train. Things got pretty wild." When I asked her to elaborate, she was cagey. I'd also asked the same question of another romance person, a senior editor who'd seen everything in the industry since 1974, and she, too, refused specifics, but said, "Those old conventions were all about the Mr. Romance pageant." Images of the old convention gatherings, which adorned the office walls, gave only hints to the events that took place there, to the Mr. Romance pageants of years past. Fabio was there, looking quite gigantic and mannequiny in candid black-and-white photos. Model CJ Hollenbach was better represented in the photos, shown fraternizing with readers, often in period dress.

CJ would later tell me that the Mr. Romance pageants were nothing but stress for him, especially the eventually discontinued talent category. Listening to some of the models crooning was "killing everyone's libidos," he told me. He also talked about his anger and frustration at once being groped by an overzealous conventioneer and how this incident was the impetus for some new and clearer guidelines. But his account of those old conventions is mostly of the fun he had with his pals, making up elaborate Regency outfits. CJ looked mean in spats. The walls of the RT offices documented this fact.

The one person who was not there in Brooklyn that day, because she was at her Texas ranch, was Kathryn Falk.

If RT, and its conference, has had a major impact on romance over the years, it has much to do with its founder, Kathryn Falk.

RT lore was almost as important as the RT itself, and Falk was the star character. I would later hear reliable sources tell me that Falk could be rather pugnacious. Once she confronted someone who'd defected from *Romantic Times* to start a competing magazine. Falk, to say the least, had not approved of this decision. And she made her disapproval known by falling hard upon the traitor, with her fists, in a hotel lobby. In the words of the person who told me this tidbit, Falk pushed the traitor down, "Texas-style, if you catch my drift. Throw down and kick 'em."

Another senior editor in the field, a sober witness whose testimony I believe completely, confirmed that these events really did happen. And she added a new, and what I would consider important, detail: Falk had appeared at that fight in that lobby with a pet chicken in hand.

"A literal, live chicken?" I'd asked this source.

"Oh, yes," she replied. "A literal chicken. Very much alive. She was going after her with one hand, and holding the chicken in the other."

There were many such tales about Falk, *Romantic Times,* and the RT convention. People said she'd ordered savage takedowns of good authors who'd gotten on her bad side, and overpraised others who had proven loyal. I heard a rumor that she'd cajoled her husband into getting matching plastic surgeries with her. It's hard to know what is real and what is made up. One assumes, for instance, that the rumors of an RT-Mob connection are exaggerated. ("They're all from *New York*, you know?" my questionable source told me.) But people believe these stories, and that itself is revealing.

Falk was also the person who would later make the controversial decision to suddenly discontinue the magazine and convention both, virtually overnight, shuttering one of the biggest names in the industry, and appointing no successor. It would be a move that shocked and angered many in Romancelandia, and which one industry person described to me as "the final diva act" of Falk's career.

When I first met the RT founder at her convention, she was circulating at the Kensington book-signing party. Falk ran her empire from the Texas ranch, but she and the dogs had come to RT that year to take a proprietary survey of the scene—which, as it turned out, would be one of the last ever. She was wearing a denim jacket, festooned with handmade patches depicting scenes from romance novel covers of yore, mixed in with some Western motifs. When I'd approached her, she'd been speaking, adoringly, of a woman who had "more curves than a country landscape."

When I asked her, with, in retrospect, comical naïveté, what kind of leader, in her view, should take the future reins of RT, she'd given me a look that said, *Do you know who I am?* "I can't imagine anyone else running it," she said. "It's my baby, you know."

I also asked her about her original goals in founding *Romantic Times*.

"Simple," she'd told me. "In those days, the men owned the big places. Some women owned small ones. But we wanted to *take* the big ones from 'em. That was the whole idea right there. Just take it from 'em." She looked at me, laughed, and ditched me to go mingle.

But that was the past. On the day I visited RT's offices, they, like other parts of romance, had become a much more serious outfit staffed by experienced romance professionals. RT conference organizer Tere Michaels, as an author, had seen her own subgenre of LGBT Romances go from a smallish group "where you knew everyone who did it" to a broad network of readers and writers across the country. "I'm constantly meeting new people who do it," she told me. "It's endless. But if you could see what it used to look like, not that long ago, you'd realize why it's so amazing to me."

When we'd met, Michaels was doing the indie thing and digging into her backlist. She had just reissued her debut book.

"It was a weird experience, for sure," Michaels told me. "But I promised myself not to change it that much—just update the technology a bit, pretty much, and to just let it be what it was. Also, my readers would *kill* me if I messed with it. And I don't mess with my readers."

"What exactly does 'messing' with readers mean?" I asked.

"Oh, the ending," she said. "I mean, other things, too, probably. Like if I cut out some minor character that people love. But, you know, the ending is the thing. The HEA. Even changing it a bit could be dangerous. I'm not going to risk it."

"What's the risk, exactly?" I asked.

"Oh, that they, the readers, will *hunt* me down? Everywhere I go. For the rest of my life. They will find me in Atlanta, or in Reno, to lemme know that they traveled *across America* just to find me and let me know that my new ending is *no good*."

"And they're not kidding?"

"Oh, no, no, no."

"Are you afraid of the reader?" I asked Michaels.

"Well . . . I respect the reader," she said, with a suddenly philosophical air. Then she added with a laugh, "But, yeah, I'm afraid of readers. If you're smart, if you know what's good for you, you live in constant fear."

It was a common sentiment among romance authors. The romance reader is feared. If you don't give the reader what she needs, you have betrayed her. If you don't fix the problem, she'll stop reading your books, and she'll try to persuade you to stop writing them, and she may well launch an online campaign to persuade others to abandon you, too. (Or worse: they'll walk onto your property to beg you to reconsider, as Annie Proulx learned the hard way, when obsessed "Brokeback Mountain" fans tried to secure her promise for a sequel with a proper romance HEA.) But give the reader what she wants and she'll buy as many books as you can physically manage to create. She will save up her money, and her precious vacation time, and use it to travel all the way to New Orleans to have you sign the thing. Everyone in publishing knows that romance readers are the world's most dedicated—for better or worse. It was a theme that Nellie returned to often when talking about romance readers. "Do not cross them," she would later tell me, once I'd gotten deeper into the field. "They will destroy you."

The fear of romance readers within romance has a particular pragmatic meaning, but once you step outside of romance, this fear is often akin to a phobia. One of the more memorable literary treatments of this misogynist fear of the "female reader" came from Stephen King, a writer who knows something about fear, and also about the experience of popular authorship. In *Misery*, from 1987, King set a gothic American rendition of *A Thousand and One Nights* in rural Colorado. His modern Scheherazade—whom King tellingly imagines as a man—was a bestselling romance author, Paul Sheldon (played by James Caan in the movie version).

In the book, this romance author is rescued from a major car crash on a remote rural road by someone who eerily identifies herself to him, through his fog of pain, as "your number-one fan." This number-one fan, Annie Wilkes (played by Kathy Bates in the film), turns out to be a sociopathic nurse who holds her beloved author hostage—just "until you heal," she keeps on insisting—forcing him to compose a romance novel to her exact specifications.

And not just any novel, but a new installment of her favorite romance series, the Misery series, so named after its heroine, Misery Chastain. Sheldon had recently killed off Misery in what he'd planned to be her final book—an experience so liberating for him that he'd popped open a bottle of champagne to celebrate. But now his number-one fan was demanding he write a new finale, in which Misery Chastain is literally resurrected from her grave, brought back into the love story, and given the proper HEA that she and all of her readers deserve. If he doesn't write this romance, that's okay, too. Annie will just torture him to death.

King's novel imagines the reader's revenge on an author who breaks the basic rule of romance: the delivery of an HEA. By killing Misery, the author was in serious breach of romance law. The reader, therefore, is entitled to compensation. She just wants the ending that is hers by right, and the legitimacy of her claim is what gives the story a deeper level of pathos and dark humor.

After his "number-one fan" has chopped off one of his feet and one of his thumbs, and gotten him addicted to pills, Sheldon manages to escape and to kill her. It would seem that the romance author has been liberated from the reader's evil clutches. But, in his post-traumatic haze, still haunted by her presence, the author hero of King's *Misery* comes to recognize that the romance novel he'd composed in captivity, the one he'd written under duress, was the best work of his career, better even than the Serious Novel he'd been working on, the novel he'd hoped would finally gain respect from literary critics. With this ending, King vindicates not only Annie Wilkes but the romance genre.

Why was Sheldon's romance superior to his more literary effort? The stakes for both reader and author were simply higher. The magic formula of romance, King realizes, isn't only about the story on the page, it is in the contractual relationship between real-life author and reader. Romance isn't about candles and chocolates, or hazy images of happiness, it's about keeping real promises, delivering the most essential services.

Legendary publisher Mills & Boon recognized the value of this principle when they were shaping the modern romance industry in the early twentieth century: give the readers exactly what they want and you will prosper, and if you decide you know better, you will perish. It was the same fear that had driven the Scheherazades of the "Writing Quickly" author panel to work more than quickly: to write so much, and so rapidly, that it was literally crippling their bodies. "The readers won't forgive me if I don't deliver this soon," one of these permanently injured storytellers had said. Industry people usually say these things as a "joke," but they're never kidding.

It wasn't an accident that King, who'd written *Misery* in the 1980s, at the height of the romance revival of the late twentieth century, picked romance for his story. The Scheherazade principle—the fine line between losing your readers and getting beheaded, or else delighting them and being lavished with gifts—is the single animating principle of the reader-driven world of romance. And this principle only deepens with the passage of time. After centuries of being maligned, marginalized, and murdered, the romance reader—so friendly in person—has only grown more angry, and more demanding of her rights.

But I think there's something else at stake for today's romance reader. There was something else, too, even in *A Thousand and One Nights*. In *Nights* we get a glimpse of life beyond Scheherazade's effort to placate her murderous audience. *Nights* may end with a typical HEA, with Scheherazade's "release from the doom of death," in the form of her betrothal to the king. But I think there's a secret second ending to *Nights,* a kind of narrative trapdoor—and, to me, this hidden HEA is what truly makes Scheherazade the patron saint of romance.

After *A Thousand and One Nights'* official HEA, after the marriage contract has been made between the king and Scheherazade, there's a second ending, a passing reference less than a line long that's very easy to miss after more than a thousand pages. But it's the crux of the story. Once Scheherazade has finally asserted her power over the king—after telling him no less than a thousand brilliant stories—she is allowed to live and also given a promotion, namely, the title of queen. We then learn that Scheherazade negotiates this offer, and that she has made one caveat: she insists that her sister, Dinazade, is given a home in the palace right next to Scheherazade's residence.

This HEA ending, between the sisters, is the resolution of a more profound romance plot in *A Thousand and One Nights*. The unshakeable bond between these women is the quiet power that has kept Scheherazade going through life-threatening tribulations at the hand of a cruel and talentless man. It's this HEA that she was after the whole time. All she wanted, really, was to live near her sister, and to live happily ever after with *her*.

And, in a way, this secret feminist HEA animates many modern romances, too. Darcy is a great character, sure, but isn't Elizabeth Bennet really after something bigger? Isn't she really seeking security for, and closeness with, her sisters? That was her motive long before she'd met Darcy, much less begun taking him seriously. And in real-life terms, isn't the story of the Brontë sisters, their real-life relationships, as compelling as the gothic romances they published?

Like so much else in the history of women, that story—of the relationship between Scheherazade and Dinazade, the Bennet and Brontë sisters—isn't fully told. But the subtle hint of it speaks loudly, precisely because it speaks so discreetly. All the stories that Scheherazade and Dinazade must have told each other in the privacy of their own palace chambers, once Scheherazade was finally done entertaining a man on the record—none of those stories is told, their existence alluded to obliquely in that one line at the end of *A Thousand and One Nights*. That coded feminist HEA is the untold story of the one-thousandth-and-second night, and every night thereafter.

That secret, second HEA between Scheherazade and Dinazade is also the animating force of RT, the true objective of its convention-goers. It's why they travel so far every year, at great cost. After the literary HEAs in their books, the real HEA happens when they put their books down and spend time with one another, and trade stories about what they've seen and been through, and what they aspire to. As with Scheherazade, the real HEA is the promise of living next door to a favorite sister—maybe in adjacent rooms at a Marriott in New Orleans or in Reno rather than in a royal palace, but no less meaningful.

This collective power of women—and the way it excludes men—is, of course, what scares people. But the women will win. That's how this story goes.

On my last evening at RT, as I fell into a heavy, drool-laden depressive sleep, my final semicoherent thoughts concerned the lingering specter of Fabio. In those days, I had a running essay, in my head, about Fabio—a theoretical Fabio "think piece," if you will. I would advance this essay, about Fabio as a culture phenomenon, a bit at a time, and I would soothe myself to sleep with this work in progress.

Like most of my generation, Fabio had been a part of my life since I was a child. I'd always marveled at him, his success, his whatever-it-is-Fabio-is. I've wondered at the meaning behind his rise to fortune.

It seemed like some kind of Big American Story. Maybe it

was a Reagan-era reactionary narrative of muscular capitalism. Muscle men were everywhere in those days, not just on romance novels. My 1980s action figures were all freakishly muscled. (He-Man comes to mind.) In baseball, Jose Canseco was starting a performance-enhancing drug insurrection that would culminate, by the '90s, in a complete takeover of the game and an arms race for the ages. Needless to say, pro wrestling was muscle-prone. (And weren't they two of a set, Hulk Hogan and Fabio?) Even the illustrations that the LDS church included in their editions of the Book of Mormon from that era, the kind handed out by missionaries, showed intensely huge muscle-bound prophets. But it's truly a wonder that a man who was a cover model *on novels* became a household name in the United States of America. His name still comes up when I bring up romance with non-romance readers of my generation and older. Fabio was just a fact of life for us. But, as the years go on, the question has only deepened: What *was* Fabio?

When I first turned to romance, I began with this question. I read a lot about Fabio. I watched videos, listened to audio recordings. And, having absorbed a fair amount of reportage and primary documents, including archival material, I had his voice in my head a lot during those unhappy early days. And, probably because of my vulnerable emotional state at the time, my thinking was somewhat overheated, even to the point of being suggestible. I may have attributed sagelike meanings to Fabio's statements.

Even though Fabio's darkness emerged in my research—his complicated relationship to his fans, his uninspiring comments about women, his rightist politics—I, nevertheless, maintained

Fabio as a muse. I don't mean Fabio, the historical personage named Fabio Lanzoni who was born on the Ides of March, 1959, in Milan, the erstwhile I Can't Believe It's Not Butter pitchman who now lives in L.A. and occasionally surfaces as a pundit on California politics for Fox News. That Fabio was not my guide. I mean a constructed voice based on the mythic Fabio. That voice, that ideal Fabio, spoke to me and guided me at that period in my life.

I contemplated Fabio's paradoxes. He has said that he seeks to "accept life simply"—and he self-identifies as "spiritual"— and yet, in the next breath, he'll chat about his 222 motorcycles. How is it possible to make sense of this? What can resolve such contradictions? Fabio himself hinted at answers: Fabio, according to Fabio, would share, without a moment's hesitation, any of his possessions. He specifically cited the 222 motorcycles. And not only that. He wouldn't care if someone borrowed a motorcycle and *crashed* it. Fabio is fine with that. That sounded potentially Zen to me. But was it really true? These weren't, strictly speaking, useful questions, but I found them useful at this time in my life.

I was also fascinated by how unlucky Fabio was in love. Or, what seemed increasingly more likely, as I read about him, that he was just terrible at love. If Fabio was really a cultural archetype, the very image of love in Reagan-era America, what did his utter failure in love signify? The more pressing question, of course, was when would I just stop thinking about Fabio already? It wasn't healthy.

Getting over Fabio, and whatever he did or did not signify, was greatly helped by meeting CJ Hollenbach at RT. Hollenbach, another male romance cover model with iconic flowing hair, was for years a fixture of RTs. All over America, he was, and still is, often mistaken for Fabio. But the folks at RT knew exactly who he was. He'd been a presence at RT over the past few days, taking pictures with fans, chatting on the lunch line, but I'd been too wretched to introduce myself. And he was, of course, also a pal of Nellie's. That was how I'd finally met him.

It was at an RT event that Nellie had organized. One of her productions. She had come to RT armed with many, many boxes of books and almost as many full of free merch. In the days leading up to RT, the hotel mailroom was something to behold. It was like witnessing a mobilization before a major hurricane or a border war. Nellie and her publisher were responsible for a good share of these boxes. But Nellie knew that cheap giveaways got old quickly. Most book promoters handed out key chains and mugs with book titles on them. Some fancy promoters handed out key chains that secretly doubled as nail clippers. Nellie went further. She arrived at RT with boxes full of pashmina, scarves that she unloosed, in full, at Devon's main event.

"I wish I'd brought more," she would say to me, with a note of genuine sadness, a rare display of emotional vulnerability that she immediately neutralized in a show of disdain for me.

"Don't even think of trying to get any," she'd added.

The pashmina giveaway had caused a near riot. Nellie was still basking in this small victory over the forces of lameness when I'd arrived to ruin it. She rolled her eyes at me from across the room, and made a big show of how disinclined she was to summon me over. She was standing with CJ, amused by my reluctance to approach them.

"You know? That guy I told you about?" she was saying to CJ, intentionally loud enough for me to hear, as I finally drew closer. "Who's creepily obsessed with romance novels? *Him*." Nellie turned to me and flashed a devilish grin.

CJ gave me a quizzical once-over, and then he gave Nellie an even more quizzical look.

I died a bit under his blue gaze. I looked away, and noticed women, all over the hotel ballroom, admiring their new pashminas and showing them off to friends.

CJ often lets passersby believe that he is Fabio. He's even signed an autograph as Fabio. "They just want the illusion anyway, right?" CJ would later tell me. "I mean, even Fabio isn't *Fabio*."

This got weird once when Fabio and his girlfriend drove past CJ in L.A. CJ just waved at them, flashing a big knowing smile. He recalled that Fabio "did not seem pleased." Nor was Fabio pleased when CJ effectively hijacked a big public appearance in Ohio. ("I mean, I had the home-crowd advantage there," CJ told me.) The crowd had so strongly desired seeing the two of them together that they had loudly demanded it. Fabio had no choice but to acquiesce. With reluctance and a big scowl on his big face, Fabio had invited his shorter, more charismatic, and slightly better-looking look-alike onto the stage. The local Cleveland media savaged the more famous model, and celebrated CJ as "Ohio's Response to Fabio!"

In CJ's telling, Fabio was "deeply unhappy" about the situation. One can only imagine the dark mood that would grip a person who encounters an uncanny and unnervingly energetic doppelgänger. What is it like to see yourself appear on the cover of millions of books, only to run into, by some kind of demonic inevitability, a three-dimensional and far more likeable version of yourself? Fabio hasn't told us, and won't. But Dostoevsky describes it in *The Double*. (I quote here from that story, substituting the main character's name with Fabio's.)

Fabio dashed headlong away, wherever fate might lead him; but with every step he took, with every thud of his foot on the granite of the pavement, there leapt up as though out of the earth a Fabio precisely the same, perfectly alike and of a revolting depravity of the heart. And all these precisely alike Fabios set to running after one another as soon as they appeared, and stretched in a long chain like a file of geese, hobbling after the real Fabio, so there was nowhere to escape from these duplicates.

Even so, Fabio kept his wits about him that day; he was a pro. CJ recalls Fabio whispering to him, "We do the handshake?" Which, CJ reports, was "like shaking hands with a baseball mitt."

At RT, when I'd first met Ohio's Response to Fabio, and shook his completely normal-sized hand, I nevertheless shifted uncomfortably under what I took to be his scrutiny. Especially with my own persecutor, Nellie, standing by.

"He doesn't look *at all* how you described him," CJ said finally to Nellie. "He's not *scrawny*. He's taller than me!"

In that moment, I felt positively buoyant. Nellie wasted no

time getting to work. When I offered her and CJ some candy that I'd gotten at the panel, she came at me.

"I'm not taking that," she said. "How do I know you're not poisoning me?"

CJ just stared, wide-eyed.

"I just got it," I said, sputtering. "It's not even open. When would I have drugged it?"

"So you're not saying you *wouldn't*," Nellie replied, "only that you *didn't have enough time*?"

Nellie was now bored. When she left us, to continue mingling ("I know you guys have *a lot* to discuss," she said, grinning at me), CJ turned to me and, with real concern, said, "Are you okay with how she talks to you?"

"Oh, yeah," I'd said. "That's very nice of you to be concerned. But I actually find it really entertaining. It's like a mean-sister thing. And, like, I don't have to go to therapy after that, you know? It's like cleansing, or whatever."

CJ just shrugged and said, "Okay, if you say so . . ."

Nellie was right: CJ and I had much to discuss. Mostly CJ did the talking. He told me of the time he was recruited to participate in an episode of *The Jerry Springer Show* as a potential sperm donor. From a pool of three hunks, a female contestant would choose a baby daddy with whom to be non-artificially inseminated. CJ, though flattered, had been too much of a gentleman to accept such a proposal.

Out of the corner of my eye, I noticed a guy in a blue jumpsuit dump a large pot of iced coffee onto a nearby fern. But CJ hadn't noticed. He was far too busy telling me stories.

For the next few days, as I watched him interact with readers at RT, it was clear that the man was a true gentleman, kind to those who shyly approached him, and beloved to his old friends in the romance community.

Mary was a very close friend to CJ. She had known him for many years and many RTs. She loved CJ and told me that when her husband's health had been in serious decline, CJ had called her every day. She was very protective of him. At the convention, she was often at his side. She'd told me that she kept watch over him. It was his job to mingle, of course, but she was always concerned that he could get himself into bad situations. Especially out on the town. He was so conspicuous with those Adonis looks and, she explained, "because of . . . The Hair." There were times when he went to bars and drunk people put their cigarettes out on his hair. "He has to be careful," Mary told me. "People are jealous. And they can be mean. And he's not gonna fight them."

Mary was an older woman who'd grown up in backcountry Tennessee, in the foothills of the Smokies. She told us stories of not having electricity in her family home for the first eight years of her life. She spoke with a brogue that appealed very much to my ears, so accustomed as they were to East Coast tones. Mary maximized vowel syllables to a pleasing effect. "Theater" was "thee-*ay*-ter." She said things like "Now, you sit your *bee*-hind right down" (which was directed at me). In a turn of phrase that made CJ almost fall off his hotel restaurant chair in sheer merriment, she referred to a certain person, whom Mary had deemed insufficiently respectful to CJ, as being "as crazy as a bessiebug." On top of all that, her email address contained the name "David

Bowie." At dinner, in the hotel restaurant, she pulled out a small bottle of homemade blackberry wine to supplement our meal.

For RT, Mary annually tailored and sewed CJ's ball costumes. This year's convention was no exception. CJ had the rare distinction of being invited annually to RT as an honored guest—an invitation that also came with some expectations of glad-handing, dressing up a bit, and showing up to help at certain events. Over the years other models had come and gone—and, sometimes because of their lackluster, or worse, performances, they were not invited back. One model apparently stood up a woman who'd won a breakfast date with him in a raffle. "She won fair. And. Square," CJ said, shaking his head. When I probed, he added: "Not naming names, but there've been some entitled assholes."

At dinner CJ told me that people forget how Fabio was himself also a romance author. But CJ definitely has not forgotten. He mocks it routinely and insists on using quotation marks when he mentions that Fabio "wrote" a romance series.

CJ, on the other hand, was a real author. He wrote a confessional memoir of his life as a romance cover model. The book, which is out of print, traces the classic story of a boy from the provinces trying to make it in New York City, "busting his ass for eight years" until his first romance cover gig, for Harper-Collins, dressed in a Highlander kilt and brandishing a gigantic sword. There were three large fans blowing on him that day. When the images were printed, "I didn't recognize myself," he said, with some wonder. He goes on to detail his time exotic-dancing, his shoot with *Playgirl*, and his appearance on *The Joan Rivers Show*. It tells of his ups and downs in the business, the people he liked and those not as much. The tone of the memoir is worldly and warm, like a close friend telling you a story. It has the voice of many people I met in the industry, self-effacing, bawdy, optimistic.

CJ is proud of this book, even though the experience was somewhat bittersweet. In particular, the responses to the book's cover, which, "as a cover model," CJ said to me, "I was obviously pretty sensitive about." Someone had said to him, "I loved your cover. *How'd you get Fabio to do it?*" It was, CJ told me, "a shot to the heart."

As he said this, he clutched his chest theatrically, and gazed into the distance. Just for my benefit, and Mary's, he struck a full romance-cover pose, right there at the hotel restaurant table, behind his uneaten dinner roll and house salad (without dressing). But Mary wasn't having it. She immediately jumped to his defense.

"Oh, hush you," she said to him.

Mary put a warm hand on my wrist and looked me straight in the eye and said, "With CJ's covers you can *feel* the emotion from the story." When there's a heroine with him on that cover, "you can *feel* the connection between them."

CJ, ever the skeptic, especially of pretension, and especially of pretension in the modeling industry, nevertheless kindly accepted Mary's praise. But he offered me a counternarrative.

"Honestly," he said, "for most of those shoots, you get a short summary of the book's plot. Sometimes not even that."

At a shoot, the big question concerned hair, he explained. Not just the mechanics of fabulousness but, more simply, what color. It had to match the hero's hair in the book. I suddenly remembered how Harlequin, for a period back in the 1970s, notoriously showed cover illustrations in which the hair didn't match that of the story's characters. It's one of the clearest pieces of evidence that romance's famous early covers were their own species, disconnected from the stories themselves.

CJ had a falling-out with the publisher of his memoir and his long-time employer, Ellora's Cave. Ellora's Cave was an upstart publisher, located near his home in Ohio, that specialized in Erotica and which had an impressive run for a bit, before going under in 2016. They'd pushed him out, he said, in search of younger "cavemen" but also because "they probably didn't love that I wrote a tell-all." (Even though they published it.) Their cover edits were the first sign that things had gone sour.

"First they put me in this bad wig," he told me. "Like, *bad.*"

Obviously they couldn't use these bad wig shots, and so they simply edited his head off the cover. In telling the story, even now, he still seemed appalled at this beheading.

The center section of CJ's memoir, of course, features a generous, nearly seventy-page gallery of images, a sampling of CJ in his many guises: as Alexander the Great, as Her Master and Commander, as various cavemen, as a loinclothed sex guy in tiger prints, or just rolling around naked on bearskins. "Calendar shot of me in my infamous purple Speedo," reads one caption. One of the lovelier images, to my eyes, captures CJ, in a candid moment of youthful brio and fabulous blow-driedness, outside the studio door at *The Joan Rivers Show*, wearing a Gold's Gym T-shirt and an exuberant smile. The image, taken by a 1980s camera, is blurry.

Also included are two photos of him and Fabio together.

One, in 1993, with Fabio at his height—and it is a height—and another from the late aughts. In both images, CJ looks mightily amused and Fabio far less so, with that Dostoevskian shadow passing over his face.

The longer I'd looked at Fabio over the years, the more, I must confess—and against my initial feelings—I did see *it*. I saw the appeal. Fabio's bone structure is monumental. It would catch the sun nicely from the roof of the Florence Cathedral. But ultimately Fabio was also limited by this, doomed to statuehood. CJ was grand because he walks among us. He didn't live in dreamland, or, like Fabio, in L.A. He lived in Ohio, where he worked as a grocery manager. He was a Don Quixote de la Akron, an actual man, with actual hair, on an actual quest.

Of the two, CJ also has the better hair. I realize this is a controversial assertion. To me, it's just true. Fabio's hair, in its day, was far above average. It certainly was well cared-for. I think it's fair to say Fabio *gets* hair, both his own and others. (To an interviewer, Fabio once said, rather slyly, I think, that the interviewer's hair "matches your face well.") Fabio made the most of what he had, hair-wise. But that hair on that head has always been rather passive and uncertain, insubstantial even, and lacking in drama.

CJ's hair, by contrast, is a symbol of his commitment to an Idea. If he wasn't so self-effacing, and constantly amused by the ironies of life, he'd probably be trapped by this Idea. He would, in that way, be truly, tragically, like Fabio.

CJ, as I encountered him at RT, wasn't just Ohio's response to Fabio, but also a response to the alpha-male type in romance generally. Making CJ the model-in-residence of the RT conference, the male face of romance fandom, was, I thought, a significant interpretative move. He wasn't a cheaper Fabio look-alike. He was a fundamentally different type of person: kind and caring, empathetic and trustworthy. CJ, not other male models, not the "entitled assholes" he spoke of, was who the women attending RT wanted to spend time with. Despite building a career on being the very image of the bodice ripper, CJ's RT tenure is a refutation of it.

When I first read nineteenth-century romances side by side with romances from today, I was struck by a major difference: those old romances were preoccupied with the plight of the heroine, her quest to achieve social standing and security. Some of them, like *Pamela,* suggested powerful backstories for their memorable heroes, but the story ultimately is carried by the heroine's journey. The best of the best, *Pride and Prejudice,* is great partly because, as its title implies, it did the work of telling the stories of both heroine (prejudiced Miss Bennet) and hero (prideful Mr. Darcy). But many contemporary romances, even though told from the heroine's perspective, often make a bigger deal about the hero.

You can see this in the titles. Romances from centuries past were often titled with just the heroine's name, or a reference to her. And yet starting with the ur-romance of the twentieth century, *The Sheik* (1919) until *Fifty Shades of Grey* (for its hero, Christian Grey), contemporary titles just as often refer exclusively to the hero. Why the shift?

Perhaps as women's social status and empowerment has increased, so, ironically, has the genre's interest in the male character—or, to put it more precisely, its interest in the problem with masculinity. It's almost as if the modern romance novelist, confident that her heroine has the world figured out, and that the world she inhabits is more open to her, is more preoccupied by a different question: What on earth is wrong with men?

This theme isn't new; it appeared in *Jane Eyre*'s Mr. Rochester, and other wounded Byronic men of the nineteenth century. Such villain-heroes still feel relevant in our stories today not because they're new, but because they seem so old and implacable. Because social and political progress hasn't resolved the problem of men but deepened it: modernity didn't make the toxic male disappear, it asked him only to hide himself more efficiently. In that way, the modern world has made such men more insidious, more monstrous. The stories of #MeToo weren't just about men exercising raw power, but about how duplicitous and creepy these crimes were—and how they weren't isolated incidents but a widespread pattern. This, I think, helps explain the enduring appeal of the gothic to us well into the twenty-first century. To defang the vampires of toxic masculinity, romance looks the beast deep in the eyes.

At RT, there was plenty of talk in the sessions about the difference between powerful male leads and what romance people call "alpha-holes." Today's aspiring romance authors are instructed, repeatedly, of the importance of this distinction.

Needless to say, as a straight male romance writer, it was doubly important for me to pay attention. The problem of masculinity was a big reason why I turned to these books to begin with: to see what women were seeing when they looked at men and their motives. Years of not understanding this subject, of running away from it, had had a damaging effect on my life and relationships.

In the lobby of the hotel, on the last morning of RT, I ran into Claire, a woman who had shared generously of her vast knowledge of romance lit with me. Because she was a romance reader, and probably read a book a day, she'd also apparently found time, during the four busy days of RT, to download and read not one but both of my published memoirs.

"I liked the first one more," Claire told me, tactfully, as we stood in the lobby of the New Orleans Marriott. "But can I give you a piece of advice?"

"Ugh. Okay."

"In both books you end up alone. In the first, the relationship story sounds like it's going well. But you just drop it. You don't actually tell us what happened there."

"A lot of readers have told me that," I said.

"Listen to them," she replied. "And in the second one, you're going through this sad breakup. Was that with the same person in the first book?"

"Yes," I said.

"See? In both books you end up sad and alone," she said.

Considering that I'd been in a divorce court only days earlier, this was the last thing I wanted to hear. So I quibbled.

"Wait," I said, "in the second one, I do end up going on an adventure with someone at the end."

"You mean that kid? The boy who's *your fan*?" she said, giving me a look.

"Yeah, I guess you could put it that way," I replied. "But that's a happy ending."

"That's not how I read it," she said. "I just finished it this morning. It's a pretty sad ending, I think. You're alone in the middle of nowhere with a stranger, you're looking for the Garden of Eden in Missouri? It's a fade-out."

"Hmm."

"So, my advice? For your third book: end up with someone. And happily. I'm not just saying that because I'm into romance. I'm saying it because *you* bring this stuff up yourself in those books. And your story will be better if you end up with someone."

"You may be right . . ."

"I am right, trust me."

"Okay, fine," I conceded. "But the thing is. Those books are nonfiction. I don't get to choose how they end."

"Yes, you do," she replied.

On my way to the airport, as I lingered in the hotel lobby, saying my goodbyes, I ran into CJ Hollenbach and Mary. Mary was telling me about various scenarios in which CJ has literally stopped traffic because of the attention he draws. She told me of cyclists and motorists and in-line skaters who've almost died or been maimed, or accidentally killed or maimed others, just to meet him. To which CJ, being CJ, had to comment, "You mean because they thought I was Fabio . . . but whatever."

Suddenly another male cover model showed up in the lobby, tapped CJ on the shoulder, and said, "Hey, they need you downstairs to hand out cookies." Without a second thought, CJ Hollenbach bowed farewell to us before turning and literally running down the stairs toward this event. But before he'd disappeared, I managed to ask him about choosing a pen name for my own future romance novel.

"Well," he said, with some reluctance, "you *could* go with 'Avio.'"

Call me Avio. Or, better yet: don't. I doubt I could pull it off. But anything is possible in romance. As my finances dried up, and as my own love life crumbled, I climbed aboard the great ship romance. It's never too late to join the community, I was told. You can live a whole life—many lives—before you become a romance author. I wanted to learn the way.

PART TWO

Travels in Romancelandia

The Barrier. The elements of the barrier can be external, a circumstance that exists outside of a heroine or a hero's mind, or internal, a circumstance that comes from within either or both.

—PAMELA REGIS, *A NATURAL HISTORY*
OF THE ROMANCE NOVEL

When I got home from RT, I felt a need to talk. I talked romance with my romance writing group, and I talked romance with strangers. Wherever I went, I looked for romance readers. It wasn't really a matter of looking, though, but simply of paying attention. They were everywhere. In a New York hotel lobby, where I was marooned for an afternoon, I witnessed a teen approach her father, a man dressed cap-to-sneaker in University of Tennessee football gear. He was parked on a lobby loveseat, among his family's packed bags, cutting deals on his Fantasy Football app. The family had apparently just ended an exhausting sojourn as tourists in New York. From what I could glean, a certain candy-selling establishment in Times Square had been the setting of a family fight.

Having now mustered up the courage, the teen cautiously said, "Dad . . . I want you to know that I don't hate you anymore."

The man looked up. Under the shadow of his baseball cap visor, his eyes seemed unfocused.

"You hated me?" he said.

"Ugh," replied the teen, throwing her head back. And then she muttered, too quietly for him to hear, *I hate you,* before turning and disappearing.

A minute later, she was prone on a nearby couch, legs draped over the armrest, deeply absorbed in the fourth and final volume of the *Twilight* series, *Breaking Dawn,* the one where Bella Dawn finally, and after so much drama, lets vampire Edward read her mind.

Almost everyone I met, fan and detractor alike, had an opinion about romance. Those who didn't read it had stories about those who did. A guard at the central Harvard library, who inspected all bags at the front desk—and who wanted me to know that she decidedly does *not* read romance—told me that there was a well-known professor who would blush and make awkward jokes each time she had to produce the most recent romance stashed in her purse.

A grad student in American studies told me that an aunt had a career as a romance author back in the '80s. "Her editor said to her, 'Read *Jane Eyre* and just keep doing *that,*' " he told me. Every day, it seemed, I discovered another person whose neighbor, or family friend, or sister-in-law was a romance author. Before RT I had been more interested in finding romance books in every corner, and after RT I was far more curious to discover romance readers, and writers, everywhere I went.

In those days, I was traveling around the country a lot for magazine assignments. Often this meant that I'd miss a week or two of my writing group. But it hardly mattered. All the world, I discovered, was a romance writing group. There were times I'd travel and sit next to a romance reader on a plane, arrive in the airport, pass a stack of new romances in the airport, then take a Lyft, in which the driver was a romance author, and arrive at a hotel, where I'd rest for a minute, then go down to the bar, where I'd meet another romance reader.

One of my Lyft-driver romance authors, whom I'd met in Chicago, was a woman who returned from war in Iraq and began furiously writing romance stories ("Aside from medical, the only good thing I got out of my service was an addiction to romance books"). When she got back from her third tour, she saved up to go on a cruise, which she'd never done before, because Sylvia Day was going to be aboard.

It was a romance-themed cruise, with author events and themed parties, and it would be full of Sylvia Day fans. "I didn't like *that* part of it," she said. My Lyft driver went on the cruise for one reason: to get some advice from Day directly, and maybe spark up a mentorship. She cleverly determined that this fantasy could never come to pass if she'd met Sylvia Day at a mere terrestrial author event. At those events, held in a hotel ballroom or a bookshop, she would have a minute and a half with Sylvia, and that was it. But in a confined space like a ship, at dinners, drinks, parties, poolside hangouts for almost a week, they would have plenty of time to get to know each other. She was certain that if Sylvia had a chance to get to know her, they could be actual friends. All of this made spending the money and the vacation time worth it for her.

So she saved, and then she went. She did all the cruise things: she sat on the deck chairs by day and did karaoke at night. The big author event happened the second day. She waited in the line to meet Sylvia Day. It was a long line. Finally her turn came: she was next.

But then something happened. She saw Sylvia, sitting at her autographing table, take a deep sigh, throw her head back, then turn to face her handler and give her an eye roll before returning, with a big smile, to the next fan. It was a small, quick gesture, but it told the Lyft driver everything she needed to know: Sylvia Day didn't have the magical formula. She was just another tired worker trying to do a job. The Lyft driver immediately dropped out of the line, still holding her unsigned Sylvia Day book.

And that was it. Though there were other opportunities to ambush Sylvia Day on that voyage—including once when it was just the two of them on the deck—she never introduced herself. Her initial calculation had been correct: a cruise would give her multiple opportunities and ample time to befriend Sylvia Day. But she didn't even say a word to her.

"She probably saw me staring and was like, Who's this weirdo, and is she going to kill me?"

"What was it?" I asked. She'd saved up for months; she'd cut back on food purchases and other necessities, just to meet Sylvia Day. What happened?

"There was no point," she replied. "I was just going to be a nuisance to her. She was there to promote her book, not to find people off the street who wanted to be writers. And I could respect that. I wasn't going to get what I wanted. So it wasn't worth bothering her. And it wasn't just that." My Lyft driver grabbed hold of the driver's wheel tightly and adjusted herself in her seat, and leaned forward in a way that somehow communicated to me that she was thinking through something and that she was reaching a conclusion about it.

"No," she said, "it wasn't just that. Now that I think about it? It's true, I was kind of sad about the whole thing. But on that ship, I got something. Meeting Sylvia Day wasn't going to change nothing for me. If I wanted to do this, I needed to just do it. It wasn't Sylvia Day's job to write my book. That was my job. I was looking for a shortcut and there are no shortcuts. I know what. Maybe once I get something published, I'll meet her, you know? Until then, the best thing was to finish the damn thing."

A moment later, I asked her if she ever talked with her rides about romance books.

"I don't talk much. And it's a funny thing, but when things are quiet, *that's* when I'm thinking about my writing. I'm the quiet kind of Lyft driver. I'll talk if someone wants to talk. But if they're back there on their phone, that's when I'm happiest. 'Cause I get to be up here, in my head, thinking about my romance plots."

She laughed.

"Yup, I'm up there, thinking about whether Janeece is gonna get with Trev, and, then I'm all thinking about *how in the world* Janeece is gonna get with Trev. And by the time I've come up with one solution—'cause I've already tried out a couple others and they didn't work out—before I know it, we've arrived at the destination. And I'm kind of disappointed 'cause I was just getting started on the problem of Janeece and Trev."

Often, when a fare would step out of her car, she would sign off of Lyft for a bit, and take a break to write for a few minutes.

She'd pull up to a curb and furiously type on a tablet or her phone the plot points she'd been constructing in her head during the ride.

"If I don't do it right away, I'm definitely gonna forget them."

She told me all of this as we drove through the streets of Chicago. And when we arrived at my destination, at a hotel off the freeway, I apologized for pestering her with my personal questions about romance.

"Why you sorry?" she said, securing the car's emergency brake and turning back to look at me with entertained curiosity. "I love talking about that stuff. It's fun for me."

"Yeah, but I feel bad that I cut into your work time," I said. "You could have worked on your story during this trip. Instead we were just yapping."

"Oh, don't worry," she said. "You wanna know the truth? Even when we was talking . . . I'm up here thinking over a plot point I'm working on. Sorry!" She laughed. "I can't help it. It's a habit."

She confessed that she'd actually had a fairly productive brainstorming session, in her head, just now while we were chatting, and that she was about to take a break to write it up. We parted there: she to her curb to write about the contemporary dramas of Janeece and Trev, and I to my hotel, to work on my increasingly gothic-leaning romance.

These encounters could take me beyond conversation, to strange new places. Even typical romance settings, like author events or industry gatherings, could lead in an unexpected direction. At an awards ceremony at an expensive, if not quite posh, Midtown Manhattan hotel, an event hosted by the tristate area chapter of the RWA, I met a woman—a reader and fan, not an author—who was headed out into the woods for a romance-themed overnight under the stars.

"It's not official. It's not an RWA thing," she explained. "I didn't make it up, though! I heard about it from a friend of mine on Goodreads, who lives on the West Coast and does it all the time."

As she described it, it sounded more like a séance. It involved seven women who would take their tents into the woods near Cornwall, New York, a town about sixty miles outside of New York City, sit around a fire, and conjure up the soul of a departed romancer.

The choice of Cornwall was no accident, she told me. It was intended to be a kind of pilgrimage in honor of the novel *Mistress of Mellyn*, which is set in Cornwall, England. The overnight was timed to correspond with the birthday of that book's late author, Eleanor Hibbert, who published under the pen name Victoria Holt.

I hadn't heard of this novel. But I was told that it was a book I ought to read. *Mistress* was considered a contemporary classic of Gothic Romance, what would likely be classified today as Romantic Suspense. *Mistress* can be seen as a transitional work in the history of romance lit. Published by Doubleday in 1960, it predated the romance boom by more than a decade; in retrospect, it pointed to the revival of the nineteenth-century craze for Gothic Romance that was to come at the turn of the twenty-first century.

But its initial success was not, in any explicit way, due to romance. Published during a time when the romance market was in ebb, the book's love plot was not central to its marketing—the cover of an early edition bills it as "the famous best seller suspense novel." But to readers then and now, it's obvious that the story's suspense, though useful for the plot, is secondary, and that it serves the larger and more central romance story. Martha Leigh is not simply trying to solve a murder, and to risk her life in the process, for the sake of solving it: she's trying to understand who this man is and whether he's a killer, because she's in love with him. The resolution of that murder mystery is directly linked with the coupling of the two main characters. Today, *Mistress* is one of those romance books that many have never heard of, and whose fans cannot believe you've never heard of.

As we stood around at the RWA awards ceremony in Manhattan, sipping on midrange champagne out of plastic flutes, I promised the séance organizer that I would read *Mistress* ASAP. Especially since I was, in my own work for my writing group, starting to become more interested in paranormal romance.

"Oh, you need to join us," she said.

"At the overnight?"

"At the overnight!"

"I don't know . . . I don't want to crash. I doubt the others want me there."

"They totally do, trust me," she said. "And anyway, I'm the boss. They have to listen to me."

That weekend I borrowed a tent, bought a bunch of supplies, and hitched a ride with one of my fellow campers, who lived in

Queens. I hadn't quite realized that we'd be pitching our tents on the outskirts of an old-timey cemetery. Sensing my surprise as we settled within feet of some tombstones, one of the participants tried to explain it to me. "They don't want us *in* the cemetery," she told me, "so this was the next best thing."

The night was spent around a crackling fire, drinking wine and eating birthday cake, and taking turns reading aloud from *Mistress of Mellyn*. It was creepy and funny and, in a way, very moving to see these readers honor a favorite author in this way.

After I'd returned from RT, from that deep dive into romance, I'd been immersed in the question of Which Genre? I had been meeting so many people who were romance fans who knew exactly which kind of romance they lived for. But I was barely committed to the romance genre to begin with: How could I really say which subgenre moved me most? These were questions that had life implications. They forced me to think about what kind of stories matter most to me, which stories I think are most true, most urgently relevant. And as someone who was trying to write romance, with the goal of publishing some, it was also just a pragmatic question. One had to make some choices and stick to them. As an author at RT had said to me, in a comment I took to be pointedly personal, "Romance authors are not commitment-phobes."

I hadn't made a commitment to genre yet. But my gut was telling me, or, more likely, creepily whispering to me: *Gothic*. Not surprisingly, realizing this only made me further disinclined to commit. But it was hard to ignore. I'd been down this road before. My first book had taken place in a prison and had dwelled on the deaths of more than a couple of people; and my second book was structured around my belief that the Book of Mormon was a work of Joseph Smith's dark gothic imagination, and had included my theory that he may have murdered a guy, stolen his manuscript (of a "romance," no less), and published it as the Book of Mormon. When I looked at it, my gothic leanings were an established fact.

The reason, however, was far less clear to me. Was it guilt tracing back to my Orthodox religious upbringing? Maybe it had something to do with being raised by a mother who was struggling with a difficult past, who had grown up in a physically and emotionally abusive household? PTSD symptoms can be contagious. Maybe it was just garden-variety disenchantment with the shallowness of consumerist culture, which does everything it can to distract us from questions about death. Whatever the source, it was getting harder to deny that my interests, romance lit–wise, were headed in the familiar direction of the dark and dreadful. I was committed to figuring out why.

Recently, for my romance writing group, I'd written a scene— not even a story, just an isolated scene—that involved a description of a person who is buried alive and who escapes this horror. I'd written it, I should say, for the group, but I hadn't actually submitted it. I was scared. It was a weird and dark scene, and I didn't want to creep anyone out, or to be judged. For that *Salon* article where I'd been asked to give tips for writing memoir— the one where the editor had cut out my advice about rejecting medical anesthesia—I had also advised potential memoirists to go to a shrink, so as to avoid the problem of their work replacing therapy, which is not good for a writer and is, frankly, even worse for their readers. I wondered if my buried-alive scene was something more for my next therapy session than my next workshop. But out in the woods of Cornwall, New York, reading a deeply, deeply creepy story under the stars with these gothrom fans, it occurred to me that maybe I should just embrace the truly horrible.

That night, I had some trouble falling asleep. Being in the woods, far from my troubles, had the effect of reminding me of my troubles. There had been some flirtatious talk at the fire, and some chemistry. And the scene now, in these tents, was somewhat charged. But I was intent on staying zipped in. I had been serially dating, and mostly to sad effect. The fact that every woman I met seemed to be wonderful, and the kind of person I could talk to and wanted to get to know better, only made me more miserable. I knew that there was no way I could enter into a real relationship with anyone at that point. The divorce had deeply shaken me. The collapse of other serious relationships had further shaken me. I'd lost good friends in these breakups. I was trying, at the very least, not to make the same mistakes over and over again.

I had been spending a lot of time with a woman, Ania, whom I'd first met in the library, while I was busy finishing my book about the Book of Mormon. During this time, I didn't realize that she wasn't a librarian but a grad student who worked for the library's reference desk. We'd spent months in that reference room, without saying a word to each other, except for the times when I'd forgotten my headphones and checked out the library's. She would later tell me that she thought I was a math grad student because of my sad fashion sense. Eventually she googled me and the first hit she'd found was an article I'd once written for *The Paris Review* in which I'd theorized at great and harrowing length on the "decline of the sexy librarian" in recent Erotica books. Nevertheless, she gave me the benefit of the doubt and we'd grown close, or, in her words, "dating or whatever." This was usually when things started to go wrong for me. So when she told me that she was planning to go to Moscow for the year, to do research for her dissertation on the literature of the absurd, I was somewhat relieved.

Surely I could give my troubles a rest for one night. I fell asleep, for three seconds, only to discover that I'd pitched my bed directly on some kind of ungodly sharp rock. The tent was too small to avoid having this rock dig into my back. The choice was either re-pitch, which would be an ordeal and also wake up the others, or I could just deal with it. After a while, from sheer exhaustion and a numb back, I passed out. Two and a half hours later, in the dead of night, there suddenly appeared a flashlight directed into my tent. Then a voice.

"*Hey.*"

I woke with a start.

"Sorry, I don't want to alarm you," the voice said. It was Kate, the organizer of the event. "But there's, um, someone, or, um, something, in the cemetery."

"*What*," I said, now fully awake.

"There's something . . . *out there*. It's been sort of prowling around."

"Prowling? On how many legs?"

"Not sure."

"Maybe we should check to see if it's one of the group?" I said.

"Already did," she said. "Peeked into everyone's tents. You were the last."

"Is everyone up?"

"No, I only woke you up."

"Oh."

"Will you come with me?"

"Into the *cemetery*?"

"Yeah."

"Uh..."

"C'mon, it'll be fine," she said.

"If it's fine, there's no reason to go. Right?" I replied, trying to keep my voice in a whisper. "And if it's *not* fine, we should definitely *not* go. So, like, either way, maybe no?"

She gave me a shaming look.

"If there's something there, we should know," she said.

"Strongly disagree," I replied. "You realize this is how every horror movie starts. They hear a sound and go toward it instead of away. Let's not be those people!"

"I'm going," she said. "Are you gonna make me go alone?"

"That's what they say in the horror movies!" I said, as I rolled out of my tent, pulled on my boots, and flicked on my phone's flashlight. We slowly stalked toward the old cemetery. It was exactly as you're imagining it. A dark, mostly moonless night. No lightning or mist rising, though. A late-summer evening, not cold, but with hints of early-fall crisp. The cemetery was small, and may have once been a church graveyard, though, if so, the church was long gone. From my inspections earlier, when it was light outside, the place hadn't seen a new grave in decades.

As we made our way in, I noticed that there had once been a stone fence around it, now reduced to traces. The forest had slowly begun to reclaim the cemetery clearing. There were more trees in there than I was comfortable with. And in the darkness, each tree stood like a thing, a presence. In short, it was eerie in a very tangible and not okay way.

We proceeded slowly. The sounds of tiny feet were occasionally heard. But nothing bigger. Then there was something. I heard it. The crack of a fairly sizable twig. Something stepped on that twig. Something large. I tapped Kate's shoulder, and she put her finger over her lips. We listened. Nothing. And then something. Another step. And another. Then we saw it. The shape of it. It emerged from behind a tree, maybe twenty feet ahead of us. It walked on two feet. A bear. Or a bear-shaped creature. It was coming right at us, slowly but steadily. Then it stopped. It saw us. I was stunned, unable to make a sound. Actually, I made one sound that was kind of consonantal choking like "chhh." I felt my feet begin to turn around of their own accord. Kate grabbed my arm and said, "Stay."

The thing began walking again. It was limping. It limped toward us. Suddenly there was a face. It was June, one of our crew. But her eyes were gone, and her face had been eaten. Just kidding. Her face was fine. She was smiling and alert.

"Oh, didn't mean to scare ya," she said, in her agreeable midwestern accent. She laughed. "Just taking a little walk. Got this bad sciatica here; gotta stretch it every few."

I turned to Kate and gave her a look.

"I checked!" she said, "I *thought* everyone was in their tents."

I don't think I slept soundly for another couple days after

that. I certainly didn't sleep soundly that night. The next morning, I pulled up my tent and discovered that the sharp rock that was digging into my back was the base of a tombstone. I'd been sleeping, or rather lying awake and freaking out, right on top of a grave. I could have attended twenty romance cruises and met every Romantic Suspense author at every book-signing event and none of it would have given me the gothic training I'd received that night, outside of Cornwall, New York.

While I couldn't sleep, with a literal tombstone poking me in the back, I had time to think. In listening to the women read from *Mistress of Mellyn* that night around the fire, one thing had become clear: it is a good idea to give serious consideration to the danger posed by the person you're in love with. In the story, of course, this question is stark. The man she loves might be a killer and sadist. The heroine spends much of the book investigating, which takes her into all kinds of dark and terrifying corners of this old creepy house. Her goal is to vindicate him, to prove that he is not the evil person he seems. But lurking not too far from this objective is the darker question: What if he *is* that villainous man? The heroine, at some level, must confront the possibility that she loves him anyway. She is forced to consider the more disturbing possibility that she loves him partly because he is so disturbed, not despite it. All of these questions, these dark possibilities, resonated with my own life.

The themes of the gothic—the divided self, the secret monster—were real things that kept me up that night and many nights. I wasn't a killer or a sadist. I wasn't violent at all. And yet I had powers. I could be charming. I could be empathetic. Was I responsible with those powers, especially when they involved other people's hearts? I hadn't reckoned with any of that, it lurked as a kind of unprocessed secret. On the surface I was a kind person, and yet I feared that, in practice, I was, as a friend and lover, just some sad reckless fool lumbering mad around his crazy, untended mansion. Was there a way out of this dark, creepy place, with its long corridors and innumerable doors?

I really wasn't sure. I feared that reading gothic stories, like those of Poe, were also part of my problem. They allowed me to see the world as haunted, period. Those kinds of gothic stories didn't dare me to see the world in any other way; they simply confirmed the hopelessness that had driven me to those stories to begin with.

But gothic stories that ended *well*—that was alluring. It took the darkness seriously, it confronted it, but also challenged me to escape it. It wouldn't let me dwell there. I could understand why readers are obsessed with Gothic Romance. "I honestly don't understand why anyone reads anything else," one of the Cornwall séance ladies had said to me. "With my books, it's like, either go big or go home." On my ride back from Cornwall to New York City I made a decision: I would, at least, muster up the courage to go somewhat big and to submit that messed-up live burial scene to my romance writing group.

I learned almost as much about romance from haters. During this period, when I was basically conducting a cross-country romance survey, some friends made for a reliable control group of skeptics. I asked an artist friend of mine, Jesse, if he'd ever read romance. His answer, without hesitation, was *No, of course not.* I asked him what his earliest associations were. "The same as anyone's," he'd said. "It's lonely women buying it at the grocery-store register." They pick one out from the magazine section because it's similarly disposable. He added a detail that was comically inaccurate: "They aren't the kind that go to the library."

He recognized that these associations were ugly stereotypes. "Let me think about it," he said.

Now, when Jesse, a Freudian at heart, said these kinds of things, he really meant it. He was serious about scouring his psyche right there on the spot, to retrieve a more precise response.

And, as often happened in these conversations, the non-romance reader, without my prompting, conjured up a complicating personal anecdote. When he was about eighteen years old, Jesse told me, he'd grabbed a book from an airport store. He didn't recognize the author or the book. But even now, almost twenty years later, he remembered why he'd chosen it. He'd bought it specifically, he said, because it was thin. To his studious young mind, an intellectual in training, a book's thinness, especially a book from an airport bookstore, advertised its literary seriousness.

"A thick book," he recalled, "was trashy."

So this young intellectual bought this highly respectable thin book, which turned out to be Annie Proulx's "Brokeback Mountain," at the time packaged as a stand-alone novella shortly after its success as a *New Yorker* short story. This was years before it became the iconic film.

Because Jesse is a close friend of mine, I instantly grasped the meaning of this airport book. Jesse had made the purchase when he was coming out. During this delicate period he had exactly three books on gay subjects, each of whose spines he'd carefully, and rather naïvely, covered with black tape and placed back on his shelf, in a tragicomic effort to conceal them from his parents' eyes—of course, it had the exact opposite effect. Jesse had never heard of "Brokeback Mountain" and he hadn't, even once he'd begun reading it, known its subject. Because the book was thin, he had just *happened* upon one of the most influential gay love stories in late-century American literature.

For my benefit, Jesse did a pantomime of his younger self, aged eighteen, on his first solo trip out of state, sitting on a plane, eyes widening as he got deeper into the story, looking around nervously over his shoulder to make sure nobody on his plane was watching him read this super-gay book. He especially didn't want anyone to see how it was making him cry. In retrospect, it was an important moment in his own narrative. I filed Jesse's story as a particularly beautiful addition to my ever-growing file of "Didn't Think They Were a Romance Reader—Turns Out It Played an Important Role in Life."

But was "Brokeback" a romance? It seemed significant to me that Jesse had identified this book in this way. On the train back from Jesse's house, I pulled out the romance manuscript I was writing. But Jesse's story lingered. Orthodox romance people would never consider "Brokeback" a romance, since it ended unhappily, but maybe there was a reason Jesse had pulled it out of his psyche.

I grabbed my phone. A quick investigation revealed what I

should have guessed: that this question is very loaded. It's one of the big controversies surrounding "Brokeback." Annie Proulx, I discovered, had been so overwhelmed by romance readers demanding that she return to the story and spin an HEA sequel that she now had deep misgivings.

"I wish I'd never written the story," Proulx told an interviewer. "It's just been the cause of hassle and problems and irritation since the film came out."

Proulx was effectively disavowing her most famous work, and in a *Paris Review* interview no less. These weren't grumpy, off-the-cuff remarks caught by a reporter. Proulx's words were carefully measured in accordance with *The Paris Review's* interview method, in which an author and interviewer spend months coediting the final version of the text. Her remarks were calibrated for their intended audience, and for posterity, and also for *The New York Times*, which quickly ran a piece with the headline: *Proulx Says She Regrets "Brokeback Mountain."* From a culture perspective, this was newsworthy. In literary terms, Proulx's words amount to a major policy statement.

"I think it's important to leave spaces in a story for readers to fill in from their own experience," she elaborated, "but unfortunately the audience that 'Brokeback' reached most strongly have powerful fantasy lives. And one of the reasons we keep the gates locked here is that a lot of men have decided that the story should have had a happy ending. They can't bear the way it ends—they just can't stand it. So they rewrite the story, including all kinds of boyfriends and new lovers and so forth after Jack is killed. And it just drives me wild. They can't understand that the story isn't about Jack and Ennis. It's about homophobia; it's about a social situation; it's about a place and a particular mindset and morality. They just don't get it."

This statement is a perfect case study in the romance-phobia that hovers around Serious Literature, the kind that Stephen King had sent up in *Misery*. If some of these fans were literally stalking Proulx's property, one could understand her fear. Nevertheless, the horror seems to derive mostly from a different form of trespassing: daring to rewrite her story.

"I figured that one of these idiots who loves happy endings would come along and start messing with it," Proulx said, of her anxiety over a possible "Brokeback" adaptation for opera.

"I want to keep the story as it is. It's a strong story and it shouldn't be mangled into everybody lives happily ever after."

Annie Proulx apparently made a terrible mistake of writing a story that readers dearly loved, one of the most important pieces of romance fan-fiction bait. As a writer I could relate to the grumpiness. But I'm sincerely fascinated by her unwillingness to fathom the meanings of her *own* story. Calling her most devoted readers "idiots" isn't just unkind, it's deficient in psychological insight, which is odd, given that Proulx is a careful and astute writer. No writer should be bullied into writing a sequel, or anything they don't want to write, but neither should they mock their readers' human needs, nor dismiss their pain.

"They can't understand that the story isn't about Jack and Ennis," Proulx had said. "It's about homophobia."

After Flaubert, the writer must trade on cruelty in order to be taken seriously. That's nothing new. Annie Proulx didn't invent that problem. But her readers are not idiots. They know quite a bit, and at quite a cost, about homophobia. And like the story's author, these readers have a message to share: *that story* is *about Jack and Ennis*. Of course it is.

How is it possible that the author does not see something important in her own work, even when it's pointed out to her? Or was that the problem? That she does see it, and that her story was, despite herself, despite her training and her conscious intentions, all along too close, for her comfort, to the logic of romance?

The very first novel printed in America was a romance. In 1742, Benjamin Franklin published Samuel Richardson's *Pamela, Or Virtue Rewarded*. From *Pamela* until today, romance has gone through different phases and incarnations in Anglo-American publishing, but it's never really been out of favor. With romance, the question has always been: Is it popular or is it *insanely* popular? For the record, we're currently in a period of insane popularity that began in 1972, with a single book. Kathleen Woodiwiss's *The Flame and the Flower*, the book that launched a million novels, a publishing industry era that might be called The Romancecene.

The popular aspect of the genre is suggested by the word "romance" itself, which comes from *romanz* a medieval vernacular language, a country dialect of Latin. In the early Middle Ages, books written in proper Latin were generally works of scholarship and theology. Whereas books written in *romanz*, the language of everyday life, and which concerned subjects slightly less lofty and often far more fun than God and natural philosophy, eventually bore the name *romanz*. Those early romances, in twelfth-century France, sometimes known as Heroic Romance, were often written in verse. They told the tales of knights and other aristocrats, and their noble pursuits of Courtly Love and noble warfare.

Real-life royals like Eleanor of Aquitaine, queen of England and France, and her daughter, Marie, actively patronized romance writers and helped these stories find wide audiences. It was good PR for their royal house, and for their aristocratic class generally, and the common people loved it.

Much history separates those early romances from ours, but there is a direct lineage between medieval knights and Mr. Darcy, who, as a stupendously wealthy landowner whose maternal grandfather was an earl or duke, was certainly gentry on the order of a knight or baronet (though, to be sure, short of a Lord). And from Darcy to our contemporary problematic cowboys and oligarchs who are redeemed by love, including characters like Christian Grey. For romance haters, there is ample evidence in this history to support the argument that the form is fundamentally reactionary. Some of the earliest books were literally royalist propaganda.

The concept of "fine love" that these stories told, that love was (literally) ennobling, and, at least through reading about them, available to anyone, eventually became called simply "romantic love." This is the idea behind pretty much every popular notion of love we have today. Not just among romance novel readers. It includes people who claim to hate romance novels and yet speak openly of seeking romance. The kind of person who loves Rom-Coms, if they're on screen, but wouldn't read one. It's probably you and/or the people you know. If you had a marriage ceremony, and lifted glasses and recounted how you met, and how you broke up and then reunited, you sang a romance tale. If you wore a white dress—a style made popular by an English royal from the Victorian period—you staged a performance of Courtly Love. And if you cried when gay marriage laws were enacted, you partook of an emotionally charged Happy Ending. The sentimental tropes of romance are so deeply embedded in our culture, we take them for granted.

By around the year 1200 the Heroic Romance emphasized not only chivalrous knights winning battles, and thus the respect of fellow warriors, but, just as often, winning the hearts of their desired ladies. These stories also contained elements of magic and the supernatural. So much so, in fact, that the genre known as romance, which grew to immense popularity over the next hundreds of years, was synonymous not only with love stories and adventures but also with spooky elements and magic personages and monsters.

With time, the taste for the supernatural, and also for aristocratic subjects, declined. By the seventeenth century, authors were distilling the magical elements out of the narrative mix, and focusing either on realistic love stories or on adventure tales. Commoners started making appearances. The Heroic Romance was, by this point, a well-known enough genre that its tropes could be used as fodder for satire. Cervantes's Don Quixote was just a regular guy who had read too many chivalric romances about knights, and who imagined monsters that weren't literally there. Which did not, however, mean that adventure and love were out of the question for him. In his pursuit of gallant greatness, and his sincere belief in the old forms, he really does embark on an adventure, where very real and wild things do in fact happen to him. That was in 1605.

As the modern novel emerged over the next centuries, readerships began to diverge. People who still unironically liked the old romances, with aristocrats and magic and Courtly Love, tended to belong to the less literate laboring classes. Meanwhile, the newly educated middle classes, who considered romance readers ignorant and superstitious, were eager for new cultural forms. These were readers who were looking for good instruction on how to look and act like virtuous citizens. Those new classes favored regular middle-class subjects like themselves, and stories that were more firmly realist and less fanciful. And often, too, stories that favored reason over emotion.

The modern novel was thus born in opposition to older romance modes. It might even be said that contempt for old romance, and an effort at differentiation from the tastes of the lower class, was central to the process that helped establish the new, emerging novelistic category of "serious literature." Though it began in the eighteenth century, this process of marginalizing romance is ongoing. It crops up all over history, in different places and times, in societies that seek to develop, for political reasons, a "respectable literature."

In my own Eastern European Jewish culture, for instance, when the Yiddish language, which had long been a street vernacular, was, in the nineteenth century, being cultivated as a "serious" language—in other words, for use by the newly educated and Europeanized middle class—literary Yiddish writers launched a war on the genre known as *Shund* (some believe that this word is related to the well-known Yiddish word '*shonde*,' or disgrace). The stakes, for the anti-romance Yiddishists, were life and death: it was about getting Jews into respectable mainstream society, where they would be safer from persecution—or so went the hope. And in the twentieth century, in Palestine, Jewish nationalists intent on reviving Hebrew language and literature, while keeping their youth ideologically oriented toward state-building, tried to have wildly popular romance works banned in Hebrew translation, their writers boycotted, and imported editions literally turned away at the ports.

But the result of anti-romance purges, in almost every case, is the same: the self-appointed authorities utterly fail at stopping the common people from reading the stories they love. But they also succeed in defining, by contrast, a high literature. The hated pop lit forms are, in the end, of great utility to people who want to be considered higher class.

And, in most cases, those higher forms cannot help but adopt elements of the trashy books they supposedly spurn. Just because the rising modern novel of the eighteenth century looked down on some elements of the old romances—the knights and the magic and the intense emotionality—did not mean it abandoned adventure and love plots with a happily ever after. That strand of literary genes thrived in the new novel form. *Pamela* and *Tom Jones* after it, in 1749, remade the love story of the romance genre into a tale about overcoming emotional, ethical, and sociopolitical barriers—not physical obstacles like in the old romances such as Calprenède's *Cassandra*, from the 1640s, in which the hero must conquer Babylon just to get close to his love interest, whom he'd seen only from afar (as luck would have it, she'd also fallen in love with him instantly, from afar). In the old magic-heavy tales, people usually fell in love instantly, on the way to other adventures; in the modern novel, achieving love itself was often seen as the quest. The happy ending, in the modern novel, was a triumph of common sense and reason, not of the emotions and certainly not of any spells or talismans.

But magical tales, like the monsters that populate them, don't ever really die. And so, before long, came the revival. By the late 1700s, monsters were back. After a brief flirtation with Enlightenment reason, readers began demanding the old-time romances. Popular love-centered novels, like *Pamela*, written by Enlightenment-era men who told moralistic tales of young ladies of good sense, whose coming-of-age spoke of their solid republican virtues, now had to compete with darker, edgier, more ambiguous, and unsettling kinds of romances. The kinds where the happy ending somehow doesn't feel truly final.

This moment in the second half of the eighteenth century, which we call the Gothic Revival, saw a major trend, in art and culture broadly, for things medieval. In literature, this meant a renewed hunger for knights, spooky elements, and emotionally charged love stories. This moment, when the romance and neo-gothic converged, is the literary genetic branch from which many of our biggest modern romance novels emerged.

Looking back on the romance tradition, and seeing how realism would continue to diverge from the gothic, there is sometimes a tendency to view the gothic strain as a dead end, to explain away moments like the Gothic Revival as peripheral to an ever-more-dominant realist tradition. But this position gets less tenable by the month, with the gothic about as alive as it's ever been. The gothic line of the novel is no passing fad, and it will never go away.

Still, the realists have Jane Austen, the master and the founder of modern romance lit. Anti-gothic Janeites will, of course, concede that Austen dabbled in aristocratic subjects, just like the old romances—but Austen's real interest, the realists would say, is with money and power and society, the stuff of realism, not fantasies of sword-fighting or nightmare plots. And Austen wasn't writing historical novels, either. She wrote about her own time, and so she came by her interest in aristocrats honestly. There is little in her stories that wasn't completely contemporary and documentable. Austen, the standard-bearer of romance, is about as no-nonsense a realist as it gets.

Austen's *Pride and Prejudice* is rightly considered the founding document of the modern romance movement. And there are good reasons to argue that most of today's romances are the inheritors of two separate modern traditions: the realist lineage via *Pride and Prejudice* (1813), and the gothic, by way of Brontë's *Jane Eyre* (1847). But to me, it's all there, both the realist and the gothic, and a visionary hybridization of them, in Jane Austen's *Northanger Abbey*.

People sometimes forget about Austen's first novel, which she completed in 1799 (though it wasn't published until after her death). *Northanger Abbey* imagines a romance reader's tendency to overread their books, to believe a bit too literally in their romances. If this premise sounds a bit like *Don Quixote*, it is: one of Austen's models for the story was a popular novel from the 1750s, *The Female Quixote* by Charlotte Lennox, a novel about a charmingly deluded romance reader named Arabella who will stop at nothing, including throwing herself off the occasional bridge, if that is what the novel in her head dictates. And what's more, her adventure ends happily.

This scenario, and Austen's, were intended as a satire of the period's powerful naysayers. An essay from 1798, published while Austen was working on *Northanger Abbey*, gives a sense of what attitudes she, and other (mostly female) novelists, were pushing against. The essay, "On the Reading of Novels," published in the London periodical *The Monthly Visitor and Pocket Companion*, claimed that novels "have a tendency to mislead the mind, to enfeeble the heart, to represent nature in improper colors, to excite, rather than to suppress, in the young and ardent, romantic notions of love, and to lead the unwary amidst the winding mazes of intrigue, and the flowery fields of dissipation . . . females, in general, are the most inclined to peruse them, and from a fatal inattention to their education, they are the most likely to fall victims to their baneful insinuations."

Austen wasn't the only novelist of the late 1700s to satirize these commonly held ideas, but her take is, of course, one of the more memorable. In *Northanger Abbey,* young Catherine makes a fool of herself by falsely claiming the owner of an old creepy abbey has shuttered his wife in the attic and then murdered her—the kind of plot twist that she had read about repeatedly in her popular contemporary gothic novels.

But, as we find out, young Catherine, though sometimes dreamy, was far from a fool to stand up to this man. Later in the story, we discover that he is indeed a bad actor who mistreats women. He may not be the twisted ghoul who tortured his wife, in the manner of a gothic villain, but the very common nature of his cruelty is what makes him an actual monster. The society he inhabits is haunted by such powerful men. In other words, Catherine's book-trained sensitivities are not wrong. Her Gothic Romance reading made her a better reader of real life.

Even though Austen didn't write in the gothic mode, at least not explicitly, she wasn't simply satirizing the gothic craze of her time. *Northanger Abbey,* like Don Quixote, was an effort to update it, to take it seriously as a form, to make it more, not less, plausible in a contemporary realist setting.

Northanger Abbey also offers us eyewitness testimony of that period's reading tastes. Throughout the book, young Catherine cannot conceal her enthusiasm for Ann Radcliffe's gothic thriller, *The Mysteries of Udolpho* (though Catherine, in her enthusiasm, also seems too busy with her own dramas to actually finish reading that long book). Catherine's love for *Udolpho* is a pure, teenaged love, familiar to us in the kind of ardor recently observed among twenty-first-century teens for the *Twilight* series. In an endearingly consistent pattern, Catherine asks nearly everyone she meets whether they've read this wonderful book, mostly because she wants to talk and gush about it with someone. But also because she wants to figure out her social world. She especially likes to quiz men on the subject, curious to learn more about the mysteries of these males, to challenge them, and to test her own social boundaries.

"Have you ever read *Udolpho,* Mr. Thorpe?"

"*Udolpho*! Oh, Lord! Not I; I never read novels; I have something else to do."

Catherine, humbled and ashamed, was going to apologize for her question, but he prevented her by saying, "Novels are all so full of nonsense and stuff; there has not been a tolerably decent one come out since *Tom Jones*, except *The Monk*; I read that t'other day; but as for all the others, they are the stupidest things in creation."

"I think you must like *Udolpho*, if you were to read it; it is so very interesting."

"Not I, faith! No, if I read any, it shall be Mrs. Radcliffe's; her novels are amusing enough; they are worth reading; some fun and nature in them."

"*Udolpho* was written by Mrs. Radcliffe," said Catherine, with some hesitation, from the fear of mortifying him.

In another scene, Catherine, walking with Henry Tilney, comments on how the landscape where they were walking looked similar to scenes from, of course, her book crush, *Mysteries of Udolpho*. "But," she says, to Henry, "you never read novels, I dare say?" Henry says, "Why not?" To which Catherine replies, "Because they are not clever enough for you—gentlemen read better books." Henry demurs. "The person, be it gentleman or lady, who has not pleasure in a *good novel*, must be intolerably stupid. I have read all Mrs. Radcliffe's works, and *most* of them with great pleasure."

In *Northanger Abbey*, in other words, Jane Austen pictures two kinds of male novel readers of that era, both of whom are fools, though of slightly different shades. There's Mr. Thorpe, who is such a fool that he doesn't realize he himself is a fan of novels, which he calls "the stupidest things in creation." The other kind of male novel reader is Henry Tilney, who is younger, and more charming, and thus hip enough to realize the foolishness of disdaining novels out of hand. He therefore must find other, more sophisticated ways to make a fool of himself. In Tilney's case, this involves offering a highly defensive, highly conditional mansplainish praise of novels. He'll concede to loving only "good novels" and only "most" of Ann Radcliffe's work—objective-sounding assessments based entirely on his own subjective feelings, and presumably those of other authoritative—that is, male—critical judgments.

These exchanges, in addition to being intensely amusing, are a useful portrait of the anxious position of men and the popular novel at the turn of the nineteenth century. And Austen was right: the younger male readers and writers in the early 1800s— the real-life contemporaries of Henry Tilney's generation— were setting a path for a male embrace of the novel, spun as "good novels," in which "good" would be defined by men like Tilney.

Scholars today have confirmed what was common knowledge back then: that until the 1840s, novels were written and read primarily by women. Many of these scholars have also noted that, starting in the 1840s, male writers, en masse, began to move into the novel form—into the genres they had once derided as vulgar and silly and unmanly, and thus dangerous to morals— because that was where the readers, the money, and the fame had shifted. But first they had to colonize the novel, to make it safe for men. Among other things, this meant removing the women. Or, rather, putting the women in their proper place.

This was the cultural setting for Nathaniel Hawthorne's letter to his publisher William Ticknor. It was 1855, five years after he'd published his book *The Scarlet Letter,* which he'd subtitled *A Romance.* "America is now wholly given over to a damned mob of scribbling women," Hawthorne wrote. "And I should have no chance of success while the public taste is occupied with their trash—and should be ashamed of myself if I did succeed." He wasn't done. "What is the mystery of these innumerable editions of the 'Lamplighter' [by Maria Cummins], and other books neither better nor worse?—worse they could not be, and better they need not be, when they sell by the hundred thousand."

And so, too, women who wanted to be taken seriously as novelists by the male establishment of that era had to make a show of distancing themselves from other women novelists. Mary Ann Evans, who published her great works under the name George Eliot, published "Silly Novels by Lady Novelists" for *The Westminster Review* in 1856. These Silly Lady Novelists were the same "damned mob of scribbling women" that Hawthorne had ranted about a year earlier. The essay, which suggested that Silly Lady Novels were dangerous to the cause of women's education, was mostly not an argument but a scathing send-up of romance lit and its tropes. *The Westminster Review* was a leftist, anti-royalist magazine, and Evans was careful to show that her trashing of books popular among the working masses wasn't simply her class snobbery. She admitted to feeling guilty for criticizing "destitute women turned novelists, as they turned governesses, because they had no other 'ladylike' means of getting their bread," but found a way to do exactly that.

Because Evans wrote this essay shortly before she published any of her own fiction, it can be seen as something of a manifesto for her later work. Like Hawthorne and many others, in other times and places, she defined her work in opposition to popular literature. But, tellingly, it wasn't sufficient in this hypersexist environment for her to write fiction in the anti–Lady Novel mode. The name on the cover mattered as much as the story itself. And shortly after she published this manifesto—anonymously—she took on a male pen name to help market her first novel.

Over the next few decades the male-dominated publishing apparatus effected a full-scale appropriation of the novel form wearing the lofty robes of belles lettres. As scholar Gaye Tuchman puts it, "by 1870 men of letters were using the term *high culture* to set off novels they admire from those they deemed run-of-the-mill. Most of these high-culture novels were written by men." As Tuchman sees it, this was a kind of literary "gentrification" process that involved an "invasion" of men into a lucrative women's field, an effort that deployed the full force of publishing's muscle to push out women and to elevate men, which ultimately shifted the balance of novelists from female to male. Not incidentally, this was around the same period that the "Great American Novel" idea, a cult of male authorship, was launched. Women were still welcomed, in mass numbers, as long as they knew their place as *readers* who paid money and homage to the Great Male Authors.

The stories told in the novels of the period gave hints to this wider conflict. There were plenty of condescending portraits of young and unworldly victims of popular female writers: the poor, devoted female readers who clearly needed the guidance and protection of the strong male novelist. This was the era of Anna Karenina and Emma Bovary, but they are only the most famous instances. There were others, including pop adaptations, what we might even call fanfic, of those books, like Braddon's *The Doctor's Wife*, which is a retelling of Emma Bovary's sad tale, but for a more prim English readership. The eponymous doctor's wife, while certainly carried away by her pop novels, doesn't dare act on her lust like Madame Bovary. Instead of falling into sin and ruination, she eventually reforms, ceases reading Silly Lady Novels—turning to more serious, male forms like history and biography—and dedicates her life to charitable acts.

During this patriarchal takeover of the novel, even long-dead female novelists were a threat. These late authoresses, too, needed to be discharged of. Jane Austen's enduring popularity frequently rankled nineteenth-century male authors. In the years after her death, her books sold better than ever in mass printed editions that were cheaply made, with lurid covers, and distributed in places like train stations, a model that we know well. Years after she was gone, her reputation was only growing. All of this vexed men so much, it gave them violent daydreams.

In the safety of his notebooks, Ralph Waldo Emerson concluded that "suicide is more respectable" than an Austen plot. Mark Twain, in a letter, confessed that though he didn't care much for Edgar Allan Poe, finding him "unreadable," he might be induced to read Poe. Jane Austen, on the other hand, was "impossible," and not just her work but her very existence: "It seems a great pity that they allowed her to die a natural death," writes Twain. Was Twain saying that Austen should have been burned as a witch? All authors have passionate views about other authors, but it's revealing that for some canonical male authors, a dislike for Jane Austen took the form of a fantasy of bloodshed.

Even as men brutally colonized the novel, there remained a strong, popular desire for female-authored romances centered on love. The women authors who'd been marginalized, and ultimately exiled from the novel, never went away. How could they? Women, after all, were always the majority of novel readers. Because of simple economics, the romance lived on. Even as it ceded ground to mainstream publishing, female-authored romance toiled along at the periphery. By the mid-1870s, publishers of dime novels and "story papers," weekly journals with titles like *Girls of Today*, were marketing romance stories to women readers. All the while, pulp reprints from romance backlists, like Austen's, continued to circulate freely.

It would take another hundred years for that scrappy, magazine spirit of those early contemporary romances to appear in the mass-market paperback, numbered and branded like magazines, which appeared weekly and monthly. And those older romances, written into newspaper copy, never really vanished, either, if you think about it: *The New York Times* today runs full courtship narratives in not one but two sections: in their Marriage announcements section and in the Modern Love column, both of which are very popular, mostly among women (many of whom "don't read romance").

By the turn of the twentieth century, the English publisher Mills & Boon, which had, at first, published just about anything, quickly discovered which genre sold best. Romances were consistently number one. By 1920, Mills & Boon was in the romance business. Their approach was simple: listen closely to what their readers wanted and provide it to them. For Mills & Boon, the customer was dictator.

Attentive writers, outside of romance, took note. One of the few arguably positive appraisals of pop romance, from outside the genre, came from Henry James, in his late story "The Velvet Glove" (1909). In this sense, James could be seen as an early pro-romance critic, a species that would become more common at the turn of our current century.

James's story can be, and often has been, read as a satire of popular romance. But this is Henry James we're talking about, and so nothing is a simple matter. In the story, a European aristocrat, a literal princess, meets one of America's most well-known bestselling romance writers, a man named John Berridge. She confesses to him that she herself has been writing romance novels under the decidedly unaristocratic pen name Amy Evans. (In a sly move, we never learn the princess's actual name.) The drama of the story centers on the princess's request of Berridge to help her advertise and promote her new "Amy Evans" romance novel, *The Velvet Glove*, a request that triggers all kinds of ambivalence in Berridge.

In the climactic moment of the tale, the princess lures Ber-

ridge into her automobile—a thrilling proposition in 1909—
and makes a power play, worthy of a romance, by dramatically
"laying her gloved hand, for emphasis, on the back of his own,
which rested on his knee and which took in from the act he
scarce knew what melting assurance. The emphasis, it was
true—this came to him even while for a minute he held his
breath—seemed rather that of Amy Evans." Berridge had made
a career writing what we now call Historical Romances about
aristocrats, and finally meeting a real princess, he becomes
enamored of her and of her duke boyfriend—that is, until she
asks him for help hawking her book in the marketplace, which
spoils his romantic vision of her.

It's a funny and revealing story about the various ways we
romanticize our lives. But in the end: Is it pro- or anti–popular
romance? One scholar, June Hee Chung, posits that Henry
James, in this story, identifies not with the Berridge character
but with the unnamed princess, the aristocrat who secretly
publishes romances under the name Amy Evans. In James's pop
romance ventriloquist act, in the romance passages that he con-
cocts and attributes to Amy Evans, Chung detects a "syntactical
similarity to James's own famously intricate prose style as well
as his way of mixing elite with vernacular diction and imagery."

It is tempting to think that James is confessing a secret desire
to publish popular romance. He was certainly gothically oriented enough. His humor here is certainly of the gentle and
admiring variety. I put "The Velvet Glove" in the same category
as *Don Quixote* and *Northanger Abbey*, stories that recognize
the power of romance tropes, and that don't see a contradic-
tion between comedy and sincerity, just as they don't see a con-

tradition between romance and contemporary realism. (I like to think, too, that James, in choosing the name "Amy Evans" for his pop romance author character, is poking fun at George Eliot, aka Mary Ann Evans, that great critic of romance.)

James set his story about pop romance less than twenty years after the word "bestseller" entered the English lexicon (the narrator of his story lingers over the gaudy red covers of 1909-era romances). That story can be said to document a historical moment, when America's cultural mass markets had become compelling enough that old Europe couldn't help but take part—a situation dramatized by the meeting between the American Berridge and the European princess—in retrospect, a prescient picture of things to come. Mills & Boon, which would eventually merge with Harlequin across the Atlantic, began operations just a year before James published "The Velvet Glove." And ten years on, the rising popularity of romance described in "The Velvet Glove" would explode into the first real romance blockbuster of the twentieth century. The notorious *Sheik*.

It's hard to overstate the influence of Edith Hull's *The Sheik*. It prefigured the outrageous global juggernaut status of twenty-first-century books like *Twilight* or *Fifty Shades of Grey*. It sold madly. It went to film in 1921, a toned-down adaptation that was a hit, made Rudolph Valentino into one of the first Hollywood hunks, and made adapting novels for the screen into a thing. It scandalized people (and, for those today who read its wildly racist and rapey scenarios, it's far more scandalous now). In its time, that wildness only helped its sales. It launched an entire industry of copycats. Fifty years later, in the '70s, it would see a revival. *The Flame and the Flower*, in 1972, the first major hit of the modern romance period, had some *Sheik* to it.

And *Sheik* copycats have never disappeared. Scholar Amira Jarmakani estimated that after 9/11, with Islamophobia on the rise, there was a dramatic rise of reader interest in the genre sometimes known as Desert Romance. At a conference in 2019, I witnessed a romance author discussing the marketing importance, to readers, of "immediate comprehension" of genre. She presented a slide with the headline: "Why Extreme Titles and Subtitles Work" and displayed two recent examples, covers of Sophia Lynn romances: *Prince's Pregnant Fake Fiancee*, which was the 2019 addition to Lynn's Royal Baby Romance series, and *Sheikh's Accidental Twin Baby Sons*, whose full listing is *Sheikh's Accidental Twin Baby Sons: A Multiple Baby Romance* (Sheikhs and Babies Series). The presenter's point was that Sophia Lynn, whose other series titles included *Sheikh's Secret Triplet Baby Daughters*, *The Sheikh's Miracle Baby Daughters*, *Sheikh's Forgotten Baby Daughters*, *Sheikh's Unknown Baby Daughters*, and others, is an author with a knack for marketing discipline. It was taken for granted that the word "Sheikh" offered readers "immediate comprehension" of genre, though the presenter, revealingly, avoided any mention of the racist nature of this comprehension.

The romance books that had followed immediately after the original *Sheik*, in the 1930s and 1940s, saw a deepening of the emphasis on the alpha-male hero, a type that seemed particularly appealing in political cultures that were growing ever more authoritarian after the end of World War I. Either in tandem with, or in response to, the spread of fascism across Europe, aggressive models of male leadership cropped up in the liberal democracies of the United States and Britain. In these societies, pop art, like comics, saw the rise of a new class of alpha superheroes, including some who we might today call liberal, but who were no less authoritarian, like Superman. In England, Mills & Boon, working to perfect the romance formula, made the "Alphaman" a key to their approach.

At the same time, romances from the 1930s, in particular, were freer than later books to challenge norms, including the institution of marriage. In the first decades after U.S. women's suffrage, romance readers were reading about heroines who were leaving terrible marriages, or whose HEA culminated with a happy relationship that wasn't a marriage. There's a romance from the 1930s that shows a woman on the cover, alone, breaking free from chains. No male to be seen.

Romance has always changed with mores, including changing meanings of marriage. During the period of revolution in America and France, when companionate marriage, based on romantic love, was considered radical and antipatriarchal, there were many more pro-marriage stories. At other times, such as the 1930s, when marriage was seen as a trap for women, there have been more anti-marriage books. And these questions are always complex: 1950s romances were conservative and pro-marriage, in the Eisenhower age fashion, but they also sometimes portrayed marriage as an arrangement that liberated a woman from a life of pointless labor in the capitalist system.

Today, in step with the times, romance isn't anti-marriage, but it certainly isn't married to marriage, either. The contemporary HEA can take many forms and is tending ever more toward less traditional relationship arrangements. I met a nonbinary person at the RT convention who was writing self-romances, about people who ended up marrying themselves.

For good reason, there remains much emphasis on the problematic depictions of the alpha hero in *The Sheik*, but a large part of the appeal of that story, to its 1920s readers, was the radical vision of a female-led adventure story, the notion that an empowered woman, who's had enough with the hypocrisies and subjugations of her life in a western democracy, can go on a solo adventure on the other side of the planet, just as men had been doing in literature for roughly six thousand years. This was a new kind of romance, in which the heroine explores the world *outside* of her society. In contemporary terms, it was a much less virtuous 1920s version of *Eat, Pray, Love*, which in a variety of ways, including its polarized reception, can be considered a nonfiction romance.

By the middle of the twentieth century, the name Mills & Boon was synonymous with romance in the U.K., the way Harlequin is to North Americans today. In fact, the Canada-based Harlequin gained that reputation because, in 1957, it purchased Mills & Boon and began reissuing their deep backlist to wider audiences. Harlequin's great genius wasn't in creating the genre but in marketing it, and in finding new ways to use the vast and busy commercial networks of North America to distribute their product. They perfected Mills & Boon's approach to cover design, turning the books into a postwar supermarket brand as recognizable and trusted as Tide or Kellogg's.

In the 1970s, fifty years after *The Sheik*, the business exploded again. The boom—the final frontier of the midcentury paperback revolution—began with Woodiwiss's much storied romance *The Flame and the Flower*. ("Their stormy saga," reads the cover, "reaches the limits of human passion as we follow Heather's tumultuous journey from poverty . . . to the splendor of Harthaven, the Carolina plantation where Brandon finally probes the depths of Heather's full womanhood.") The book, unprecedentally smutty for a mainstream release, was a giant hit. A second book, in the subsequent year, *Sweet Savage Love*, by Rosemary Rogers, was such a megaseller that it launched a new subgenre. Many romance readers today know of the Sweet Savage subgenre but probably don't know its source.

Why the 1970s? Romance fiction is of particular interest during periods when sexual politics are of pressing concern to people, or, as scholars describe it, "renegotiated." The 1970s, characterized by the rise of Women's Liberation, among other radical social movements, was certainly one such period. This could also explain why romance boomed in the 1920s: *The Sheik* was published at nearly the same moment that women's suffrage went into effect. The *Fifty Shades* phenomenon of our time can be debated in a variety of ways, but it's hard to deny that the heart of the story, the question of its heroine's consent—dramatized as a plot over whether she'll sign a contract—surely tells us *something* about our current moment and its sexual politics.

What about the alpha-male type, which continues to be prevalent not only in the form of Christian Grey and his ilk, but in a host of aggressive shapeshifting heroes that populate the ever-growing Paranormal genre? Many feminist critics argue that a reading of these characters as "glorifying" aggression against women is not only incorrect but contains an implicit misogynist bias. It tacitly assumes many women simply aren't sophisticated enough to know what is harmful in real life and what is fantasy. It misreads why and how many readers use fiction to think about the world.

Today's romances, particularly those by younger writers and read by younger readers and critics, tend toward a more openly progressive and even radical feminism. Romance has long been a way for women to imaginatively manage power issues of patriarchy. Certainly its history has proven its ability to hold radical potential.

The notion that all Women's Lib era feminists hated romance is not entirely correct. In a 1973 edition of *Ms.* magazine, queer activist and writer Adrienne Rich published a vigorous defense of *Jane Eyre* against its critics, past and present. "Always a governess and always in love? Had Virginia Woolf really read this novel?" Rich asked. She concluded that Brontë's genre-defining romance novel offers us "an alternative to the stereotypical rivalry of women; we see women in real and supportive relationship to each other, not simply as points on a triangle or as substitutes for men." As for Brontë's HEA plot: "Marriage is the completion of the life of Jane Eyre . . . but it is not a patriarchal marriage in the sense of a marriage that stunts and diminishes the woman; but a continuation of this woman's creation of herself." Even those second-wave feminists, Rich's contemporaries, who hated romance (Germaine Greer said that romance fans "cherish the chains of their bondage") never dismissed it as frivolous: they understood its very real political power.

And it's no accident that Adrienne Rich focused her attention on *Jane Eyre*. Romance's most political stories often take the form of the gothic plot. Today, even non-explicitly Gothic Romance stories are gothic. *Fifty Shades* is a good example. Technically it falls into the Erotic Romance subgenre, and lacks any explicitly gothic material. But it grew directly out of *Twilight*, the gigantically influential vampire romance series (that lacked explicit sex). These two books are a perfect study in how genre works because they're directly linked by way of fan fiction. E. L. James first wrote and published the story on a *Twilight* fan-fiction forum, in which she took the basic characters and scenarios of the original story, keeping the basic drama, while swapping out certain features and scenarios. It's like taking an engine from one car and putting it into another. What matters most, really, is the engine, not the frame.

And while the frame of *Fifty Shades* isn't a paranormal story—Christian Grey wasn't a vampire, *officially*—the engine of the story is still fundamentally paranormal in that this hero is deeply, dangerously abnormal. The implausible old-time Gothic Romance tropes of *Fifty Shades* make more sense in this light: for instance, Anastasia's virginity is an old staple of gothic lit, not a realistic element given her social background as a twentysomething college grad living in twenty-first-century Seattle. Tropes like that, in fact, remind the reader that it matters little that this story is taking place in modern America. This "worldbuilding" technique makes the story more suggestive, largely because it leaves the gothic unstated while clearly signaling it to the reader. Similarly, this world's hero, Christian Grey, who may seem like your typical rich prick, is, from a formal perspective, basically a vampire. What is an oligarch if not a very skilled and well-groomed bloodsucker? Fans of the book know his lineage, and it colors their reading of the story.

Ours wouldn't be a gothic moment if the dark elements of these stories stayed put, safely contained, in their genre. Like a vampire nation, the gothic subgenre propagates in the general population, hiding in stories where it doesn't belong, darkly concealing its influence in plain sight, lurking around, masked. Just as Jane Austen, in *Northanger Abbey*, shows that her heroine's gothic fears are ultimately justified—especially when those fears center on male violence—our contemporary culture maintains a gothic streak in order to realistically represent a world of patriarchal violence, and to answer the difficult question of how love and relationship are possible in such a world.

From the eighteenth century until today, the romance has, through its gothic visions, dealt directly with a central problem of modern existence: how the hetero male, privileged in patriarchal society, can be simultaneously an object of love and understanding and security and yet also a source of pain and subjugation and abject fear, how a figure from the dominant class can be both hero and villain. The vampire is the great hero of our age because ours is still a morass of patriarchal rape culture.

The current gothic revival is itself undergoing a new wave of young romance readers, especially by way of the young adult (YA) category. For them, the gothic offers possibilities that sidestep traditional modes of femininity and masculinity. The gothic mode has always challenged social norms, revealing them to be a web of self-deception, and these revelations underscore that truth must be plural and nonbinary and queer. Today's gothic subgenres, especially Paranormal, in which any and all varieties of bodies are given their due, prove fertile ground for the kinds of identity narratives that are most relevant to today's young readers. The queer revolution in romance, long coded within gothic subgenres, is just beginning to emerge.

The boom in romance lit is also a boom in critical writing about romance, not only among academics and culture critics—some of whom also write romance themselves—but also in the press. Within the span of a few months, *The New York Times* ran a sexist, condescending, and ragingly ignorant "roundup" of current pop romance literature, written by a male grandee of publishing, but it also finally hired a serious pop romance columnist. It was a belated hire to many romance readers, but it signaled that there is a younger generation at the *Times* who is starting to get it.

Many of today's feminist critics argue that Second Wave critics got romance wrong by characterizing it as simple Reagan-era conservative propaganda. Some critics hold that their critical forbearers, especially those who were using sociological studies, survey-type research, lacked good data and that their conclusions therefore were far too reductive. I tend to think of critics from the 1970s and '80s as mostly just dated—but largely due to their own success. They weren't entirely wrong about what they saw, even if they overstated the case sometimes. But their ability to identify and describe the ideological problems in romance has, I believe, helped romance writers confront the industry's problems. It is a slow process, but the feminist criticism of old is, if anything, only recently coming into its own.

If past academic work claimed that romance fixated on traditional gender norms, there is an argument to be made that today's romance, for that same reason—its centering of gender identities—is uniquely prepared to lead the way in rewriting those norms. And as the relationship between academia and the romance industry has grown, with more and better research efforts, and also with more romance authors themselves doubling as scholars, the questions of literary politics have become much more central to the way romance publishing is practiced.

But the question of good data continues to vex. What are the facts of romance? How do we measure the influence of these books on our politics and society? It is the thing that has bothered every romance alarmist in history, but the underlying questions seem valid: If these books are so popular, how exactly are they affecting people? Is there a way to document this effect?

Everyone recognizes, for instance, the "bodice ripper" cover, an artifact from 1970s novels that became common currency. But what are the facts behind its ubiquity? Scholar Jayashree Kamblé, returning to the archives, argues that the publishing record proves that rape-hero books—the ones whose narratives, between the covers, were truly bodice rippers—fared poorly with readers in the '70s and that these outliers disappeared quickly from the market. But the covers remained. And they transformed the romance industry, yielding a visual language that would go on to adorn millions of books, and remain the image of romance stamped on the minds of people outside of the genre. The bodice ripper became, in a sense, a design concept that suited the needs of publishers' art and marketing departments even as the narratives themselves were literally telling a different story. (If there's any doubt that "bodice ripper" was more of a marketing than a literary category, consider the term "bonnet ripper," which has been used to refer to the chaste books of the recent Amish subgenre.) In Kamblé's account of it, those covers attracted romance readers not because they offered an image of male violence but because they offered the exact opposite: male violence neutralized.

Conclusions of the kind seen in one recent scholarly paper, published in the *Journal of Gender Studies*, demonstrate the dangers of analyzing romance data. Based on a tiny sample size of a few recent Harlequin and Mills & Boon books, the author concludes that "the formula of popular romance fiction temporarily incorporates elements of modernity (in this case, signals of feminism) but maintains its 'boy meets girl' storyline. This leads to the conclusion that these romances purport to adjust to twenty-first-century ideas but have not shed their essence."

The problem with this argument is contained in the argument itself, which shifts terms from "popular romance fiction"—a very wide category—to "these romances," which seems to refer to a far more narrow grouping, to only the few Harlequin titles examined by the author. Even if the wolf-in-sheep's-clothing argument applies, that "these romances" were slyly appropriating feminist tropes for a regressive agenda, does it really mean that we can confidently say that the "formula of popular romance fiction" *in general* takes this approach? It's a big leap. And it's not exactly supported by the evidence presented in that paper.

And, in the current publishing field, it's a leap that seems harder to make, given the millions of romance readers, including the younger ones, who spend much of their time and money on romance books that don't do that at all. We are being asked to ignore too many counterexamples.

One thing is certain: any conclusion that says romance, or any genre, possesses some kind of immovable "essence," as the scholarly article puts it, is unsupportable. These things shift all the time. They can alter radically. This is not just my view. There is a strong trend toward romance-positivity in criticism these days. In fact, they have a home of their own: the peer-reviewed *Journal of Popular Romance Studies*, established in 2010, just in time to absorb the cultural tidal wave of *Fifty Shades of Grey*. Culture commentators, who write for magazines, are also more likely than ever to adopt a sympathetic stance toward the genre. The anti-romance article cited above, which was published in 2019, may well represent a minority opinion at this point. But almost all sides agree that romance matters, and so the debate is alive.

When I asked Nellie whether I might sit in on a cover art meeting at Devon, she agreed under the condition that "you don't say a word. Not *a word.*" And so, only days after the *Mistress of Mellyn* séance in the woods, when I'd slept unsoundly on top of a grave, I found myself in a boardroom in Midtown Manhattan, watching how romance covers are made today.

The meeting involved the art director, designers, and editors who'd gathered to discuss an upcoming season of Devon book covers, everything from the merits of pearlized paper and embossing, to printable foil covers, to cowboy outfits.

Outsiders to romance typically only know, and tend therefore to obsess over, romance book covers. But even as I was becoming less of an outsider, my interest in the covers only increased. On the one hand, they seemed entirely self-explanatory. They weren't meant to be mysterious, but instantly legible and decidedly memorable. As a system of signs, romance covers work almost too well, which is why they've convinced non-romance readers that romance covers can tell you *all* you need to know. But the more I read romances, including old ones, and saw how much the stories diverged from the tone of their covers, and the more I learned of the history of romance covers, the more I realized that the covers, precisely because they are misleading, are more nuanced than people give them credit for.

It seems odd to use the word "nuance" to describe the cover of, say, Shelly Laurenston's *Bite Me*, which features a half-hunk, half–Siberian tiger staring out seductively from the cover. But open this cover and things get interesting: in a note directed personally to the reader, Laurenston, who is also the author of the bestselling *Bear Meets Girl*, apologizes for the tiger, since the hero of the story is, technically, a tiger-grizzly hybrid. She knows that her readers will object, but "there's only so much pressure I can put on a design team," she pleads. "Creating a cover that can successfully get that across . . . that's a bit of a challenge." Concludes Laurenston: "There's only so much an artist can do," implying, of course, that the writer's art surpasses that of the visual artist. Thus she concludes, somewhat slyly, by celebrating the art of the novel over visual design, an artform that, unlike fiction, is "unable to conceive of the wonder that is a grizzly-Siberian tiger male with a honey fetish and introvert tendencies."

I'd never seen an author open her book with an extended apology to the reader for her book's cover art. It seemed like a uniquely romance move, in which an author is in direct and open contact with her readers' needs, slightly terrified of their reactions, and also cleverly able to play on this intimate bond to solidify it further. In this case, Laurenston and her reader are members of an embattled tribe of misunderstood Paranormal fans (outsiders to the genre, she suggests, don't "truly understand the wonders of the hybrid nation"). There is a dance happening here between romance author and reader, genre and publishing platform, a world of signaling that the uninitiated simply miss when they stop at the cover.

Comedy is also part of this signaling. Outsiders think romance covers are funny. But what they often don't realize is that romance readers agree, and that humor is a large part of the intended appeal. For all of its heartfelt earnestness, romance is a comic genre, and its fans are there for laughs. A popular item of *Smart Bitches, Trashy Books,* one of the most trusted magazines in romance, has a column dedicated to mocking romance cover misfires.

The aspiring romancer in me was eager to see and hear the conversation among the professional artisans, the people who made these covers for a big publisher and who were working within a robust art-historical tradition: the genre conventions born of a century of romance cover art, walking the line between received wisdom and innovation.

When I asked Nellie for a peek behind the scenes, she just rolled her eyes and said, "I guess." For the people at Devon, it was a routine weekly meeting. For me, it offered a series of clues.

The meeting was run by Devon editor in chief Jack, who wore his casual dress intimidatingly well. Before the meeting began, I'd asked him what genre one should choose, if one wanted to break into the field as an author. Without hesitation, he said, "Amish." Then laughed. And said, "Not sure that's your thing. But it's everywhere." That year, he told me, Devon had published Amish titles every month save one. There were no upcoming examples being reviewed at the art meeting on the day I visited. "Come back next week," Jack had said, "we can talk horses and buggies then."

At the art meeting, Jack's signature was a cup of Siggi's yogurt and a bottle of Perrier. When the Siggi's top was rolled off, it meant the meeting had been brought to order. Proposed covers were presented by designers, and discussed with editorial and marketing, as Jack held forth.

"The maid looks angry," he said, examining a mock-up for one forthcoming cover.

"She's supposed to be angry," the designer replied.

"But she looks *really* angry."

Next.

Jack examined a cover. He was visibly bothered by a certain vegetable.

"That's a tough cabbage there," he said, tapping on an image of lettuce.

"I think it's a lettuce."

Jack didn't reply. Instead he became contemplative. The designer nodded and made a note. The next cover proposal was presented. An Urban Contemporary.

"I really like her," Jack said. Then paused. "Mmm . . . but she's too eighties."

"Eighties is back," someone offered.

"Exactly," Jack said, already glancing toward the next selection. "Until it's gone again. We don't want to have to repackage in two years."

Next up was a Western Romance. On the cover was a solitary, super-chiseled cowboy leaning against a cattle fence. His cowboy getup was immaculate, possibly brand-new, and appeared to have been freshly pressed only minutes before the shoot.

"Oh, I *like* him," said one of the designers.

Jack narrowed his eyes.

"Is this one the twin?"

"Oh, yes, he's the *bad* twin."

From my own preparations for this meeting, I knew that this romance featured the bad-boy doppelgänger of an earlier, more straight-edged cowboy from this series.

"Can we line up the covers from this series?" Jack asked.

The group now considered four nearly identical cowboys. But there were character differences. In one book the cowboy hero was ambivalent (as far as cowboying was concerned), whereas later in the series, the cowboy in question was unorthodox in his commitment to cowboying. Needless to say, these various cowboys' commitments to love were also in question throughout the stories—that is, until their endings. The only clear visual difference between the good cowboy and the bad seemed to be the latter's black hat. And this was either a good move or not. Jack seemed to be unsure.

"Maybe there'll be triplets," said one of the designers.

"Which guy is he twins with?" Jack asked. The designer pointed to the twins. "Biological?"

"Pretty sure."

Jack inhaled loudly. He was satisfied. For the moment.

"I'm gonna return to this one," he said.

A cover featuring a shattered plate was presented. Jack immediately shook his head.

"We've already had something like this," he said.

Nobody seemed to remember it. But they didn't question him. A designer sitting next to me whispered in my ear, "Jack has a ridiculous memory."

He was on to the next cover.

"It's subtle," Jack was now saying. This was not a compliment.

With the next cover, he drew in a big yoga breath and closed his eyes. And with eyes still shuttered, he exhaled fully. "We should think about whether the glitter here is too gloppy."

"Doesn't [author name redacted] love glitter?"

Jack's eyelids flew open.

"Don't worry about her," he said. "Also, let's think about trade for this one, not mass market."

A book cover was introduced as "Oh, this one is repped by the same agent as the cat book." This comment prompted groans of recognition around the room. In me, it elicited something like low-grade dread. It seemed like a cautionary tale for an author.

That cautionary tale deepened. The group was vexed by a

cover that involved a suspense plot. Nobody liked the cover, which looked somehow smudgy and yet also overly realistic, an almost toylike rendition of a remote camp on a frozen tundra.

"We're selling the threat and it's not coming across," Jack said. "We need a new approach here. What's the plot of this one?"

"The North Pole," someone chanced.

"There's something under the ice," Barry, the book's editor, added, sleepily. "Something terrible."

Jack nodded and said, "Okay . . ."

". . . a monster, or maybe an alien . . ."

"From another planet?" Jack asked, firmly.

Barry nodded, though he seemed unsure.

"Is it green?" Jack asked. "Could we do a glow thing?"

A designer started scribbling.

"Not sure," Barry said, with a sad sigh. "The manuscript isn't in yet."

I felt a pang of writerly empathy with this author whose manuscript was clearly delayed. But God bless Barry, the book's editor, who spoke up for his author. He asked that the author be consulted about any changes to the cover.

Jack pursed his lips at this request.

"Well, her self-pubbed covers are pretty over-the-top. So maybe that's not the way to go."

I had to pipe up with a question, hoping Nellie wouldn't find out that I'd spoken.

"Is author input on covers *ever* welcomed?" I asked.

Jack smiled, with what I took to be a mixture of amusement and pity.

"Rarely," he said, with a note of finality. "We had this author who wanted this really subtle literary cover, but we said, 'Look, if you let us put a cat on this thing, we could get your book into Walmart.'"

A few minutes later, when another book's editor relayed a message from her author—"She wants dollar bills hanging from the trees"—everyone sighed.

Jack turned and looked right at me and said, "*This* is why we don't ask for author input."

While I always like having that voice in my head, of the skeptical Manhattan editor in chief, the fact remained that I was very much in search of author input. Soon I was traveling again. This time through Colorado. And, as always in those days, I checked the local listings for romance events. And, as sometimes happened, a romance event led me to unexpected places.

It was a night like many in the vast empire of Romancelandia. There were three featured authors. Two I'd heard of; one I hadn't. They read a bit, but mostly just chatted and played to the crowd. There were handouts and books, and a raffle, and maybe a couple of other crowd games. It ended with an autograph line. I never tired of these events. But, like any industry product, they were fairly cookie-cutter.

Some vendors out front tabled for various romance-related companies. There were people who specialized in book cover design for indie authors. They could create something to your exact specifications, and if you were just a beginner, they could help with every aspect of the design, including helping you hire a photographer. Another vendor was working on an app, he said, for book clubs, to help keep track of reading and conversation, and to help the readers share comments with one another, in real time, as they read.

Another vendor, who had no table, was circulating in the crowd. She seemed to be unofficial. I watched her going around, making her pitch to people. She had a business model for selling indie books that guaranteed "significant sales." The service claimed to be a consultancy for aspiring authors, and that's how they marketed themselves, but it seemed, to me, more like a bundling operation, in which they bought an original manuscript at a flat fee, produced it into a product, and promoted it with other products on Amazon's platforms. From what I could tell—and they were vague about their contract's terms—it seemed that the manuscript, once sold, belonged entirely to them; it was unclear to me if the author would see any royalties. Was this one of those author scams? Was this woman that notorious pudding-monger I'd been warned about at RT? Would she abscond to the hills of Carolina once I paid her?

As the featured authors were signing their books I met someone in line. It was a long wait, so we got to know each other fairly well. At some point she'd said to me, "How would you like to meet a real ghostwriter?"

That was how I met Tina (not her real name). Tina was, to be specific, a *former* ghostwriter. My friend from the line was a good friend of Tina's. I had told her that I was on a mission to write romance, and also to write a book on romance. This had sparked an idea. This woman believed that Tina was something of an unsung genius, and that she had never gotten her due ("Not just saying that because I'm her friend. It's just *true*," she assured me). She wanted Tina to receive some public notice, even if it was as a ghost. The match was perfect, she said: I would get an exclusive conversation with a semifamous ghostwriter, and Tina would at last attain some form of public acknowledgment.

As we stood in the shrinking autograph line, she texted with Tina. Tina seemed reluctant to agree to this idea but finally relented ("I always tell her, you *need* to do an interview"). The meeting was set for the next morning, at Tina's home, outside of Denver.

The long driveway leading up to Tina's house was a shrine to bears. There were statuettes of bears resting against trees, and branches, and one glorious life-sized carved wooden statue of a grizzly walking upright. The slower I drove, the more bear-related things I saw on her property: bear engravings, weather-beaten crocheted bears, and totemic objects that I was guessing were also bear-related. If you stopped for a moment to look at any given spot in her yard, there was a good chance the image would eventually resolve itself into a fat-rumped, small-headed outline.

The very first thing she said to me, when she opened her door, before hello or welcome, was a slightly defensive "So I guess you know about my thing with bears, huh?"

It seemed like a test. I chose my words carefully.

"Well, I like bears, too," I said, which was, strictly speaking, true. "And anyway, I support any serious collection of anything," which is also something I do believe.

"Well, okay, then," she said, and cracked the door open more, though still not quite inviting me in.

"What *is* your thing with bears, though?" I asked. "Just out of curiosity."

"They're like these incredibly vivid versions of people. Like people who are lost in the woods, or something. Some people think of them as ancestors, or as humans who've transformed, or souls who never finished their quest."

We were still standing in her doorway. I began to wonder if maybe this insight about bears *was* the interview, and that I'd have to search this one statement as the answer to all my questions. Perhaps sensing my anxiety, Tina opened the door and stepped back to welcome me.

She was smallish of stature. This was important only insofar as it seemed important to her. She mentioned it a lot. During my visit, she referred to herself once as a "spark plug" and on another occasion she said, "I may be small, but I know how to take up space!" She strutted around her cottage in black jeans and an unbuttoned denim top with a few rhinestones on the trim over a white T-shirt. The sleeves of the denim top were rolled up at a rakish angle, and she wore a million bangles that clanged on her wrists and invested her gestures with the enchanted gusts of wind chimes. In the many photos of her around the house, she wore her hair blown out rather magnificently in long waves. But when I dropped in on her, her hair was pulled back in a ponytail. Her nails were painted a shade she described as "palatinate purple."

Tina had ghostwritten for a major author until about ten

years ago. She never met the author because the author was dead. She wouldn't tell me who it was. Tina was honor bound not to utter the author's name.

"For a while, I *was* her. I was the trans version of her."

Tina brushed off the question of when she transitioned.

"I don't think of it like that. I've been transitioning my whole life," she said. "But I didn't really come out, openly, I guess you'd say, until I was in my twenties."

In the past, she rarely revealed to her professional collaborators that she was trans. But she suspects that some knew. "If this was happening today, I may have been able to be more open. *Maybe*. It's still no picnic, believe me."

Today she runs her own business on Etsy. She still does some writing occasionally, but nothing serious. As for being a romance author, she considers herself retired from that line of work. But, recently, in the past few years, she has been toying with the idea of coming back, maybe even writing a romance with a trans protagonist. She wasn't sure. But she was thrilled that, for the first time, it seemed possible. Even so, this theoretical comeback posed all kinds of challenges: it would be hard for her to write as herself, for instance.

"The truth is, in the last years, I got so used to ghostwriting. You do it so much that it actually starts to feel like it's your own stuff. When years of the storyline *are* yours, how are you not gonna feel like that? So when I think about writing again, I just sort of automatically assume I'm ghostwriting."

As a ghost, in the early years, she'd read the books that her author had already written, and kept a journal in which she tracked the characters, plots, settings, and themes. Sometimes, it read as a kind of diary in which she would muse about these characters as though they were people in her life, people whose mysteries she was trying to understand. Ultimately it was the author herself that Tina was trying to grasp.

"It was like trying to crack a code. I wanted to keep all the details straight. But it was more than that. I also wanted to understand how it all worked. What was that, I don't know, core thing that made these stories *hers*."

Tina also went directly to the source, collecting information on the life of the author.

"I studied every interview she ever gave for clues. I spoke with her family, and asked them all kinds of questions. At first, they were a bit leery, you know. But then we met one afternoon, we rode horses—they could see that I knew how to saddle a horse, which they liked—and we drank and had a good old time, and finally one of them says to me, 'So why do you want to see Mom's letters, anyway?' I told her that if I was gonna write stuff that did any kind of justice to their mother's work I had to learn more about what made her tick. Those below-the-hood type things that are right under the surface of the stories, too, but that you really can't quite see when you read them. Until you learn some details from the life, and then you can't *not* see them in the stories, everywhere."

I asked for an example.

"Oh? Let's see . . . the desperate desire to break free from a repressive home. That whole thing . . . It's in the stories she wrote, but it's also something she knew about from her own life."

A few drinks into our conversation, I asked Tina about the

writers she liked from the early 1970s, a literary scene that I was curious about.

"I'm gonna stop you right there," she said. "Let's just put it like this. The thing you need to know about me is that my writing hero is . . . *Jeraldine Saunders.*"

Tina paused, with an impish look on her face, patiently waiting for me to join in on the joke. When she detected, in my face, not a glimmer of recognition, Tina performed a theatrical sigh of disappointment.

"Please tell me you at least know what *The Love Boat* is? Or else I'm gonna feel *ancient.*"

Of course I knew *The Love Boat,* I told her. This news came to Tina as a deep relief.

I used to watch reruns back in the early 1990s when I watched daytime TV at my grandparents' house: *Bewitched* and *Gilligan's Island, Scooby-Doo* and *He-Man*. Episodes of *The Love Boat* made it in there, too, but I had mostly found it boring and overly adult for my young tastes. It gave me the distinct and unpleasant feeling that I wasn't getting the joke. Still, I had been drawn in by the hairdos and mildly terrified of and generally titillated by the show's underlying 1970s sex dynamics.

I didn't know, until Tina told me, that the show was based on a book, *The Love Boats* (1974) by Jeraldine Saunders. Saunders had worked on the wild orgiastic cruises of the Swinging '70s and she had written the definitive tell-all.

"I adored her," Tina told me. "I wanted to *be* Jeraldine Saunders. She was this hilarious, boisterous, glam, scrappy, sexed-up adventure gal, right? Who gets rich telling her *dirty stories*? I mean, yes *please*. That's the dream, isn't it? I was ready to sign up. It's the reason I became a cruiseaholic. And a writer."

I asked her how much the show resembled the book.

The book was more smutty and gossipy; the show had to be cleaner for the TV audience. But the basic idea, that she was the first female cruise director, was real, Tina told me. "That's actually what Jeraldine Saunders was. She was a true badass, that Jeraldine! And then she writes this book, which became a major hit show, and she goes around telling people about how it's gonna be in reruns until the day she dies."

This same Jeraldine also liked to claim that she single-handedly saved cruise tourism, back when the industry was in steep decline, when all of the fabulous midcentury oceanliners had become dinosaurs, decommissioned as vessels of transport after the airline industry became big. Saunders apparently liked to boast that an executive at Princess cruise lines, her former employer, had told her that she'd single-handedly caused the industry revenue to jump three thousand percent.

"I thought that was pretty groovy," Tina told me. "At that point in my life, Jeraldine was one of my idols, I would say."

Tina stopped herself. Fearing, it seemed, that she might be getting into the weeds with me on this subject.

"I'm guessing you're not a cruiseaholic, are you?" she asked me.

"I wouldn't describe myself as that, no."

"Well, I don't wanna bore you with my old coming-of-age stories."

I hastened to add that if I wasn't a cruiseaholic, I sincerely was something like cruise-curious. I mentioned that I was considering going on a cruise for romance readers. A romance industry promotional voyage, the kind that features romance authors and their fans. She knew exactly of what I spoke, though she hadn't been on one herself, not wanting to mix business with pleasure. I mentioned my former Lyft driver from Chicago, her quest to find, and eventual disillusionment with, Sylvia Day.

"Your Lyft driver was right; it ain't worth the trip," Tina said, getting up to take a smoke. "Unless you're a cruiseaholic. But if you're just going to meet authors? Even if you do corner Sylvia Day, somewhere in the middle of the ocean, what's she really gonna be able to tell you? And I'm thinking about this, as an author, and how I would feel being on that ship, with those fans, and not being able to get off. It sounds like a nightmare. I'd be so irritable! I go on cruises to be left alone, not bothered. That would probably be one of the worst times for a fan to approach me. God help that poor reader who tries to talk to me when I'm on a cruise!"

She laughed her smoker's laugh. And speaking over her shoulder, as she made her way to the patio, Tina added, "I guess that's why I'll never be invited on one of those cruises!"

Tina stood on her back patio, puffing on her Marlboro Lights, petting the head of one of her collies who was nuzzling for attention. With cigarette in mouth, she stretched and gazed at the shifting light over the mountains on the horizon. I stood, too, next to the couch in her living room, and grabbed my phone to do some research. When Tina sat back down, I was in possession of some additional info on Jeraldine Saunders.

I mentioned to Tina that, per my searches, some critics had said that Saunders was a bit of an exaggerator, that she wasn't exactly the *very* first woman cruise director, even though it was rare in those days, as it still is. Also, that claim of a three thousand percent rise in cruise revenue might have been somewhat questionable. Even if true, she was surely a bit fast and loose about taking *all* credit for that bump when, of course, it was the TV show, not the book, that was the huge hit.

I suddenly felt bad for rattling off these fact checks, like a fun-killing know-it-all. I was not certain why I was doing it—my excitement about the subject, and wanting to get to the bottom of the mystery that was Jeraldine Saunders, was probably to blame. But if Tina was bothered by my comments, she forgave me. It seemed that she was even amused by my new enthusiasm.

"Well, I didn't know that stuff, but it's interesting. Now that you mention it, I'm not surprised at all. I mean, yeah, of course she played up her hand. She was a hustler. That was the thing I loved about her. If you'd told me back then, 'Oh, you know Jeraldine exaggerates! She wasn't literally the *first* woman cruise director,' I would have said, 'Good for her, then!' To me she was a model of ambition, of doing things your own way as a woman in a man's world. She *might as well* have been the first woman cruise director. In my book, she is. And she was, without a doubt, the greatest!"

I thought for a moment whether I had any role model quite like that, as a writer. For a moment, I thought that maybe my role model should also be Jeraldine Saunders. It's true that I hadn't yet read *The Love Boats*—and that I'd only first heard the name Jeraldine Saunders minutes earlier—but Tina had really made the case, I thought. And wasn't Saunders's story, in a fabulously 1970s kind of way, a pop feminist addition to that tradition of American boat lit that I liked so much, a disco version of Melville and Mark Twain?

As a reader, Tina still loved the old stuff of romance, the Regency books. It never ceased to fascinate me that so many romance readers come back to Regency. Why? Was it simply because Jane Austen wrote only six complete novels and that simply isn't enough for us?

"I think it's more than that," Tina said. "If you're a woman in society today, there's all kinds of rules that govern you, what you can say, read, think, how you can dress and wear your hair. And especially what you can do. The catch, though, is that these rules are not stated. In my opinion, that makes them crazier than in old times, and in a way, more random and cruel. We live in very complex times for that reason. Regency settings have as many rules as we have today. The one big difference is that the rules are much more clear, and the roles, socially, are much more defined. That's very useful to women, I think, to be able to understand the game, the rules of the game. So I don't think women are escaping into a fantasy of old times: they are just using those settings to figure out the present. And when you think about it, contemporary romance does that, too. They look at our world directly, but they describe its rules and all of that, almost *as though* it were remote, like a Regency setting, where these things are clear. It helps us sort things out."

As someone seeking out romance for its rules, I could relate. I was particularly interested in that last phrase: *It helps us sort things out.* Can Gothic Romance also help us sort things out?

"Well, it has to, right?" Tina replied, right away. "If it's a romance, there has to be an HEA. And that is always a sorting out. But, I agree, it doesn't quite go as far in sorting out the world. And it does a lot of unsettling in the process. Too much for my tastes, that's for sure."

These days, Tina reads nonstop. And she's even joined book clubs, but without revealing her identity. ("I'm there as a civilian," she told me.)

"When I retired from ghostwriting, I was doing pretty well. I mean, that's *why* I stopped. Also, because it was killing my back, literally destroying my body. I aged out of romance writing, I guess, before I did serious damage. I sound like I'm some kind of old boxer or something, right? If I didn't take these hikes every day, I probably wouldn't be able to walk. I need to be able to walk in the mountains every day."

I asked Tina about gyms and she just laughed. "Can you imagine me in some outfit like that? I can't do any of that gerbil-on-a-spinning-wheel stuff. I need air, and trees, and my dogs."

Did she have any co-ghosts?

"There were a couple of us. Over the years, I'd say another two. And maybe one or two more who helped cover on some."

"Who was the primary ghostwriter?" I asked. This gave Tina a big belly laugh. She threw her hands around, creating a gust of chiming bangles.

"Depends who you ask, I guess. I would say, 'me,' of course." (More laughter, more chiming.) "But, if I'm being honest, I'd say I was the primary, at some points, and, I guess you'd call it, the secondary at other times. But that's not how it went. We never used those terms, 'primary' or 'secondary.' It was always teamwork. And a lot depended on what was going on in our lives, how much time we had, how much work we needed. Who needed some extra cash."

One year, Tina's stepdaughter had health issues, and she also needed to make a major repair on her roof. She asked for more work and her publisher was able to give it to her.

"I think everyone was happy as long as there were some checks to go around. Other than that, why be competitive? Hell, it was *fun* to read the books of the other ghostwriters. It was like seeing your own story move forward on its own, like you were just sitting there at home for a few months and all of a sudden the next book in your series just appears, like magic."

The other ghosts, Tina explained, would do something interesting in the plot, or with the characters, something she had never thought to do.

"It was great fun to read. The best part of all is that you get to respond to what they did, when it was your turn to write. It's a bit like playing music together. When it's going well."

And when it's not going well?

"It can feel like two steps forward, one step back. Someone takes the story in a certain direction and you just groan to yourself, 'I don't love this direction, and it's going to be a drag to move the story through it.' But honestly that kind of thing was rare. It happened at the beginning, a bit, before we figured things out. Eventually we'd look over each other's manuscripts, before anything went to print. You know, consulted with each other? Like if one of us was stuck, or if you had an edit, like if something wasn't making sense, or just wasn't working, the other would say so. It was actually a great way to work, like having an editor who's as deep in the story as you are—which is very rare, since what editor has time for that? There were times when we'd chat over the phone—'cause we lived like five states apart—and we'd just gossip about these characters as though they were our close friends, which they were, in a way, and a lot of the stories and plot twists and details came out of those chats on the phone. I loved it. And you see what I mean? It wasn't really competitive. It was like a team. We're all sharing that name."

Tina's small online store "does pretty well," but it is the romance money from those years, plus work designing clothes and jewelry, that helped give her the necessary financial freedom. That ghost gig was the game changer for her.

"I was lucky," she said, and then caught herself. "No, that's not it. I was *good*," she said with a laugh. "I know that sounds like some showboating. But it's true. Just want to be clear about that! I wasn't run-of-the-mill. I was damn *good*—I could spin a hell of a yarn. And I've always been a great liar. So I wrote good stuff and I wrote *all the damn time*. And I delivered my manuscripts on time, to the minute. I got that ghostwriting gig, to begin with, because I had the chops. And, by the way, I had some sales before that gig, too. I was a star, I tell you," she said, flourishing her hand out, mock-diva-style, issuing forth a chiming breeze toward her mountain backyard.

"Well, maybe not a star. But publishers knew me and

respected me as a pro. So I'm not denying my talents or abilities here: but, yes, I also got lucky. I knew lots of others who had the chops, too, but didn't catch a break. Some of them did okay, but a lot dropped out. So, yeah, I stuck with it, with grit and all that, but I'd be lying if I said that I didn't think about quitting all the time. All the time. You had to, if you didn't already have family money or something. And, to be totally honest, I might have quit fifteen years earlier, too, if I hadn't gotten that break."

Even before she had any success, she was keen on pen names. Later, when she had more success, she was even more into pen names.

"I'd read romance my whole life and I knew many—some of the ones I liked most—had been ghostwritten. To say it didn't bother me is not even true. It didn't even cross my mind. I mean, it's not like I was ever going to meet the author, right? It was just a name on a dust jacket. I imagine this is different today. But back in the old days, it was much more normal for an author to be this faraway thing, not even a person."

When she became an author, even before the ghostwriting job, her thinking shifted: she wasn't merely neutral to pen names, she actively embraced them. "I got why it was so liberating. For me, it was privacy. I was always very close with my neighbors. Still am. We chat all the time, and check on each other. They know very well that I used to write romance novels. But never did they know what my publishing names were. And they never will! And there have been people closer to me in my life who didn't know at all, or only later found out, that I'd begun doing ghostwriting. Those pen names, and being trans, too, were things only my closest people knew. But, in truth, there was almost nobody who knew my pen names. There were more people who knew that I was raised as a boy than knew my actual pen names."

I asked if she ever considers returning to the field.

"Oh, hell no!" she said. "Unless, maybe, I will. Ha! I mean, I'm still deep into it. I've been reading romance since age nine. Probably writing since about then, too. It's not a habit I'll ever break. There are some advantages to not writing. I'm reading more than ever these days, more than I could when I was writing. I'm still reading all the newest stuff. I still love some of the classic genres, but this new stuff that's coming out? These twenty- and thirtysomethings? writing about . . . *everything,* all genders, the *whole* story, and all kinds of genre bends, and all kinds of new readers, too. It's so, so exciting to see.

"And it's true, reading some of this stuff, I get that old impulse to sit down again and do one of my own. Some people would say that's jealousy and maybe they're right. But it's more about the excitement of creating something new, my version of it, and then sharing it. I've even sat down and started a couple new stories. Just not sure if I want to . . . or have it in me . . . to go the distance. There's a part of me, you know, that never got to tell *my* story, my full identity. But we live in a time when that seems more possible. So, yes, a small part of me is saying, 'This is it, babe! This is your chance to tell *that* story.' It's very tempting, believe me. And the money, of course."

The time had come for Tina to take a walk with her dogs. The dogs had so mastered the art of reading Tina that the moment her couch creaked a certain way, they were off.

We walked over Tina's patio, into her backyard, to a trail head at the edge. From there, we continued into a sparsely wooded forest.

"You know that Bezos guy?" she tells me, as we walk on the path. "He not only steals all of our books, he also stole the symbol of feminism: the Amazon."

"The warrior woman?" I asked.

"Yup, that's what I mean," Tina said, tossing a stick to one of the collies and watching him jump.

Tina tells me that Orellana, the Spanish conquistador who named the Amazon River, gave it that Greek name after the powerful resistance he'd met there from the river's indigenous peoples, especially from bands of warrior women.

"I'm not sure how historically accurate that is, but since there's some disagreement about it, I like to think that Orellana died when his ship was attacked by women. It's gonna be the same for Bezos. When he goes down, it'll be because women bring him down."

Tina laughs, and her bangles chime along with her.

"Well, it's a good story, isn't it?" Tina says to me, as we continue our stroll down the trail. "Or maybe it will be a different story."

We stop suddenly, to listen to a bird call. When we start walking again, I ask her how the story of Bezos's downfall would go if it were a leftist revolutionary romance. Tina thought about it for a moment.

"Well, the real revolutionary story would be about two lovers who first meet when they're on an undercover mission to assassinate an evil billionaire. Or maybe just take him down legally, if you want to keep it more civil."

We walked some more. And then she added, "But I dunno . . . maybe there is hope for a real Bezos romance? Obviously he could be a vampire. Yeah. Maybe love will somehow open the locked casement of Mr. Bezos's heart. It would need to be something more realistic than Christian Grey, I think. Maybe one night, unable to get any sleep—money can't really help you sleep, you know—the Bezos-type guy thinks to himself, *What is the deal with all those romance books that I sell and make gazillions off of, anyway?* So he picks one up, reads it, and it changes his life."

Tina unfurls the whole plot, right up to its HEA. The Bezos character opens up to love. Even after getting super-rich and, arrogantly, driving his marriage into the ground (this was a ripped-from-the-headlines plot, since the Bezos divorce was in fact hot news at the time). Yes, he decides to try again. But he doesn't know how. His efforts are cringeworthy and bad. Finally, because of a mishap at a party, where a woman mistakes him for someone else, he realizes that he's in love. He doesn't know that yet, because he's a man, but he does know that he's intensely drawn to this woman who has no idea who he is. He realizes that he'd been living a lie, as a tycoon. If he has to mask himself in order to be seen, to be loved, then he's been living a lie, hasn't he?—he realizes all of that. He chases the woman down and, after some twists and turns, they end up together. Having found true love, and recognized that his life is a lie, and his wealth has been a force for evil, he elopes with his lover and gives most of his wealth to the revolution.

"The story ends with him speaking at a rally of striking canning-plant workers?" I asked.

"Maybe," Tina said.

Tina picked up a stick from the side of the trail and tossed it off. One of her collies, deer-like, leaped over rocks and fallen trees in pursuit.

As we watched him run through the forest at a slightly frightening pace, Tina said, "But I'm thinking about it more, and I've decided that I like the version of the Bezos-like character getting taken down by Amazons more. Let the HEA belong to two of the Amazon women, you know?"

After these trips into the romance heartland, I always returned home to Boston excited to reunite with my romance writing group. Having seen some of the variety of life in Romancelandia—that the abundance of romance subgenres truly did represent a diversity of humans out there—I also began to better understand the members of my local writing group: where they fit into this big picture. And where I might, too.

When we'd first met, or rather when I'd first joined the group, and we'd gone around the circle introducing ourselves, I'd detected some subtle divisions. But I hadn't quite understood what it was all about. Now, after RT, and after some months of reading and meeting people, I was beginning to get it. The divide traced itself along genre and generational lines.

The three millennials were into Paranormal, and the two over-fifty women were into Historicals. Naturally, Aparna, our leader with her ever-present vape pipe, was a Paranormal fan ("the more messed up, the better," she explained to me), while our other leader, Janice, had been reading Historicals "since early on," though she qualified this preference by adding that she was "always trying to stay aware of the latest trends."

This last statement, an elder trying to be diplomatic, nevertheless elicited knowing grins from the younger members of the group. Aparna kept her own counsel, except for a series of short, rapid, squirrelishly impatient puffs of vapor.

Within the group, Aparna set the terms of the conversation. She once declared a certain piece of writing praiseworthy by virtue of its being "low-key savage." She said the word "sexy" a lot, and she pronounced it *sucksy*. If she said, "That's actually pretty *sucksy* (puff, puff)," in reference to something you wrote, it meant you were on the right track. If something was *mad sucksy* it made your whole day.

Janice wasn't low-key savage, she was just low-key. Her hair was long, parted, and perfectly symmetrical. She probably hadn't smoked anything in her life, except maybe a Christmas ham. She wasn't a prude, once you got to know her. But she definitely didn't refer to things as *low-key savage* or *mad sucksy*. When pushed, she might concede that something was "yummy."

Aparna and Janice were the kind of duo whom people meet and ask: *So how did you become friends?* The answer, it turned out, was that they were both nurses at a local hospital. They'd bonded on one late-night shift over a shared love of Anne Rice books—though not the same Anne Rice books. They agreed on little else, genre-wise. But it was enough, and soon Aparna and Janice also discovered that they each dabbled in writing romance themselves. Thus was born this on-again-off-again, casual but serious, romance writing group.

One other thing they did agree on: an aversion to medical romance.

Medical was a genre that I was curious about, albeit disinclined to actually read. It is one of the biggest in romance—Harlequin has an entire line dedicated to it, with its own colophon and six monthly releases. The Medical genre traces back to the middle of the twentieth century, before the romance boom, and, along with Historical, Western, and Gothic, has become one of the mainstays of the industry. (Harlequin recently closed its Western line, a reminder that even some of the most reliable genres are not forever.)

Medical is particularly tied to our zeitgeist. Post-WWII, when women entered the workforce en masse, romance plots were fueled by the dilemma of love and marriage versus career (a strict binary that later feminist critics despised). Romances of the 1950s began to take place in offices or other workplaces, often between male bosses and their female subordinates (another reason critics hated them). By the '60s, a hospital was as common a setting for romance as a manor or abbey. It offered high-stakes drama, and yet was a relatable experience. By the end of that decade, the market was so saturated with doctor/nurse romance that readers demanded more exotic locales, and those medical romances found their way to every field hospital in every remote jungle and mountain range on earth.

As the medical profession has continued to grow and to employ an increasingly large percentage of women, so Medical Romance has become one of the major romance genres. There was a recent Harlequin series called London Hospital Midwives. Titles feature the now-commonplace doctor heroine: *The Surgeon's Convenient Husband, The Nurse's One Night to Forever,* and *Melting the Trauma Doc's Heart.* And the genre hybrid: *The Sheikh's Doc's Marriage Bargain.* Another Harlequin title from this crop reflects the perennial need for exotic hospital locales: *His Surgeon Under the Southern Lights,* which takes place in Antarctica.

Though many of their fellow nurses and techs read Medical Romance—and some doctors, too—Aparna and Janice did not. They were not opposed to it, per se. "Well, actually," Aparna added, "I'm like borderline opposed to them. And you're not gonna catch me ever reading those Harlequin ones"—she turned to Janice and gave her a semiapologetic look—"not being a snob or anything. I'm sure some of them must be okay, but yeah, not for me."

Janice might not have appreciated the jab at Harlequin, which she sometimes defended, but she agreed that Medical was not on her own list, either. "I've read some," she told me. "It's fun sometimes, you know, to see what they get right and wrong. Some of the mistakes are pretty funny. But it's true, when I read I don't want to be in hospitals more than I already am."

But Military Romance, for Janice, was another story entirely. She read Military voraciously, and she also wrote some of her own. Janice herself had served in the Navy. And she came from a Marine Corps family. The Civil War monument in the New England township where she lived included the names of three of her family members. Military personnel can buy romances in the commissaries, so there is a distinct segment of romance readers and authors today who are ex-military people. At our first workshop we discussed her latest.

Janice's Military Romance was also a Historical. Set during the Civil War, the story featured a woman from Baltimore, a mixed North and South city, who operated as a Union double agent. But that espionage setting was background to the real story, her heroine's reason for putting herself in danger: to be close to her fiancé, a Union soldier who may have been taken prisoner of war—or so she'd heard. The story was full of understated drama, and of honest, precise descriptions of grief and longing. In the end, even amid the pain of loss, the couple is reunited. There was not a dry eye in the room. Janice was thinking of expanding it into a novel.

I found these kinds of stories intimidating to read. These women were writing fluently in their native language, while I was struggling at basic comprehension. I learned a lot in those sesssions. Mostly by writing romance that didn't work. The women of the writing group pointed out the flaws in my stories. "It honestly just seems like a lot of the time, you go for a laugh when you could say something real, heartfelt," Janice had said. "I think the stories would be better if you did that."

I resisted the strong desire to reply with something "funny."

Janice, possibly out of pity, added that sometimes my efforts at humor did work. Like when the heroine of one of my Viking romances teases her Viking lover about how comically huge his arms are. That kind of humor worked, she explained, because it helped the reader see the characters better, and established a power dynamic between them, lifting her up and bringing the Viking down to size, so to speak. But then there was another romance hero of mine who realizes that he is in love when he hears his lover fart from the other side of a log cabin.

"Just no," Janna had said about the plot-critical fart.

"Really? I thought that was kind of *sweet,*" Linda said, in my defense.

"I *guess?*" replied Janna. "But . . . just *no.* No farting in romance."

This seemed to be the consensus of the group. I took this consensus as law. I was an eager disciple. And I appreciated good, solid Pamela Regis–style principles like that.

After the fart-class meeting ended, Janna approached me, to clarify her criticism. "I like your stories," she said, "but I agree, I think there's something blocking you from, I don't know . . . talking *emotionally?* Maybe I'm wrong about that. But it's something I think about when I read your stories."

"Yeah," I said, "it's a huge challenge for me."

"I don't think the humor is necessarily a problem—except for the fart," she said. "But if you're using humor to replace true emotions . . . that can't happen."

I was also having trouble with real-life romance. Things were going alarmingly well with Ania, the woman from the library who wasn't a librarian but a grad student in Russian literature. On a summer day, walking together on the boardwalk at Brighton Beach, she had asked me if we could hold hands "just until that bench," and pointed to a bench probably twenty feet away on the boardwalk. We tried it. She took my hand and we walked a few paces before she let go, with a sigh, even before we'd reached the appointed bench.

What was wrong? The problem, she said, was that this felt so right to her. It was making her sad and angry to feel good about me. Later, when I'd asked her what she'd been thinking at that moment, she'd said, "Ugh, that divorced *douche*bag."

But, as in my written romances, there were also some signs of progress. I was, for instance, learning to literally embrace the post-sex rush of oxytocin, that crazy infusion of chemicals that makes us want to bond with another person. This had always scared me. Now that I was trying, in my life, to confront my fears and past mistakes, I was making a conscious effort to stick around—both literally, by just staying put, and also emotionally, by not mentally distancing—during that chemical bonding.

And in doing so, it immediately became clear why I'd spent my entire adult life fleeing the scene of sex. The feelings involved terrified me. The full emotional spectrum was there, exposed raw. Everything from the earliest feelings of being a small child, held and comforted, to the feelings of being an adult at the height of health but with twinges of awareness, at the bone level, of aging. And the hardest part: the flesh-level vulnerability of it, the helplessness. The desperate drive to put my head against her head, my cheek against her cheek, and glue it there. The oxytocin bonding thing felt as literal as a desire to make my head glued to hers, literally fused one to the next. That feeling was so strong and it scared me.

But in allowing myself to experience this, in feeling all these emotions and in letting myself do the glue thing with our heads, I felt better than I had in recent memory. Alive and strong and hopeful in a way that I hadn't known, if I was being honest, ever. Even so, I could never admit to my girlfriend that I was feeling these things. I definitely couldn't admit to her that she was the reason.

But I was starting to write about these emotions more persuasively, especially in fiction about other people. I was finally writing some decent romance stuff. I wrote a story about a woman who works in a circus, who falls in love with a fellow performer. Together they undertake the old act, the Woman Who Is Sawed in Two, but really it was about intimacy. It was hokey but also kind of good.

"Okay," Aparna said, when it came time to discuss this circus story. "This one was *mad* sucksy."

It still wasn't quite heartfelt, though.

When I brought my first Amish Romance to my writing group it immediately raised eyebrows. Vikings was one thing. But Amish, that was new.

"Amish is really hot right now," Aparna said, matter-of-factly.

"Nobody has any idea why," Janna added. "And *I'm* not gonna read it."

"You'll read *his*, though, right?" said Janice, our ever diplomatic co-leader. Janna made a face.

The collective reply to this first submission was summarized by Linda, who declared it "very informative." The others, grasping for something positive to say, agreed that I had done quite a bit of research on the world of the Amish. I was applauded for trying "something different."

Then I brought another Amish Romance. And another. People were whispering. But they were being pros about it. In therapy, I discussed my motivations for this sudden Amish turn. My therapist believed that it was a way for me to talk about the Orthodox Judaism of my upbringing. This was true. Whatever part of my brain stores my thoughts and feelings about Judaism is the same part where fiction writing lives. Who can say what this might mean, psychologically, but it is undoubtedly the case. And on a conscious level I knew I wasn't going to write about Orthodox Jews, because that didn't fit comfortably into mainstream romance genres.

Amish had seemed like a good compromise. In the world of romance types, Amish offered me the kinds of Jews I wanted to write about. And not because of the beards and black hats, but because of the questions about faith and the modern world, the questions that come about from living in an embattled minority that emphasizes practice and group loyalty. The taboo of dating outside of the community, the question of leaving a patriarchal world and being shunned as a result—all of these questions resonated with my upbringing. There's a joint meet-up group in New York City for ex-Amish and ex-Orthodox—this is not a coincidence.

I myself have commiserated with ex-Amish people. Once, at a party, someone asked me if there were things I missed about being Orthodox—a rare question: usually people want to know "why you left"—and I gave a detailed description of how much I missed the serenity of the Orthodox sabbath. This person told me that he was happily ex-Amish, but that there was a part of him, the rhythm of farming, that he could never really have back and it was a source of sadness for him.

As it happens, there was also a more literal Amish overlap

in my background. Having grown up in Ohio, my Orthodox summer camp, where I attended as a camper and staff member, was in Sugar Grove, Pennsylvania. The summer camp had cultivated close relations with its Amish neighbors for decades—the campers and staff were well acquainted with generations of a few nearby Amish families. Some of the most formative experiences in my Orthodox childhood contained an Amish twist to them.

When I worked on staff at the camp later, the head counselor and one of our Amish friends would sometimes conduct language experiments, with the Jewish guy communicating in Yiddish and the Amish man replying in Pennsylvania Dutch. Both are dialects of German. As a young person, I found this to be a mind-expanding exercise, almost a kind of parlor trick. As an adult, I can recognize it as a fascinating historical convergence between two religious minorities, persecuted in Europe, who made their way to America, where they cross paths one summer day in rural western Pennsylvania, with two of their youth eating Popsicles together and tossing their ancestral languages around like a football.

Why not just write Jewish characters? I was told this was too niche. It seemed weird that Jewish was niche but Amish was not when we're both less than one percent of the population, but so it was. There have been some Jewish romances in the past. You could include the wild success of Leon Uris's *Exodus* in 1958, which isn't technically a romance but, given its ending, could arguably be seen as an HEA in the service of hyper-nationalistic propaganda. (Tellingly, it was the biggest bestseller since *Gone with the Wind* in 1936, another book considered borderline romance.) And there were some isolated Jewish titles later in the century. Today writers like Rose Lerner and Shira Glassman are doing Jewish Romance. Sarah Wendell, founder and editor of the much-loved magazine *Smart Bitches, Trashy Books* wrote some Jewish stories. ("Just in time for Hanukkah!" as she told me.) But, just as often, writers who work with Jewish themes in romance tend to bury these elements in books that aren't marketed as Jewish.

I did once overhear a hip romance editor at *Publishers Weekly* say, during a meeting, "Why *aren't* there any good Hasidic romances?" But everyone in the room knew it was an idea that seemed plausible only at *PW*'s office in New York and that it wouldn't play much in most of the country. The words "Jewish is really hot" have yet to be uttered in a romance setting.

It could happen. And if it does, it will probably be driven by the same market forces—namely, Christian readers—that have made Amish hot. Because, ultimately, the genre has far less to do with its Amish subjects than its non-Amish Christian readers, both evangelicals and casual Christians who take their Christianity in the lighter shade of Inspirational. These broad-ranging groups are the ones who determine this particular market.

I'd heard talk about Amish at romance gatherings all over the country. Sometimes people would laugh off the genre when I mentioned it, but very few hadn't heard of it. When I'd asked her what was hot, Nellie had a box of Devon's latest crop of Amish Romances sent to me with the note "Here you go, perv."

In just a few years, Amish Romance had exploded. According to an Amish Romance expert, Valerie Weaver-Zercher, whose 2013 book, *Thrill of the Chaste: The Allure of Amish Romance*

Novels, was itself an indicator of the popularity of the field, the genre, formerly a niche subgenre within Inspirational, took off in 2007, with fourteen major titles (not including indie books). Five years later, it had shot up to eighty-five. By the time the editor in chief of Devon had advised me to go Amish there were, on average, two major Amish titles published per week in the industry. The big genre sellers, Beverly Lewis, Wanda Brunsetter, and Cindy Woodsmall, had, at that point, sold a combined 24 million books. Amish Romance is now a broad category of its own, large enough to sprout its own subgenres. Weaver-Zercher offers this excellent catalog of them:

> You can read an Amish-themed romance set in
> Pennsylvania, Ohio, Indiana, Kentucky, Oregon, Colorado,
> Missouri, Kansas, Montana, Maine, Wisconsin, or Mexico.
> You can have your heroine young, youngish, or middle-
> aged, single or married or widowed. You can have her
> Amish, formerly Amish, soon-to-be Amish, soon-to-be-
> not-Amish, born Amish but adopted by the English, born
> English but adopted by the Amish, neighbor to the Amish,
> or snowbound with the Amish. Within inspirational
> Amish fiction, you can now find Amish Historicals, Amish
> suspense, Amish Wild West adventures, Amish cozy
> mysteries, Amish quilting novels, and multigenerational
> Amish sagas. One author is writing, at the request of her
> editor, "Sassy Amish," or what she called "Urban Amish"
> (these are "totally not your mom's Amish books. Except for
> the Amish. They're still there"). Another hopeful author
> is writing "lighthearted romance with an Amish flavor."

There is now Amish paranormal fiction, thanks to Ruth Reid's 2011 novel that folds an angel in the Amish cast and to *Plain Fear*, Leanna Ellis's Amish vampire series. And while you shouldn't expect to find these down at your local Christian bookstore, you can now read Amish romance novels of a quite different orientation. Yolanda Wallace's 2010 *Rum Spring,* which narrates the love between Amish teen Rebecca Lapp and English woman Dylan Mahoney, joins three series featuring gay Amish men to create a growing corpus of LGBT Amish romance.

If I was serious about getting published in romance, it made sense to find a subgenre that was growing. I wasn't used to being particularly pragmatic in life or as a writer—for instance, I became a writer—but, if I was going to have a shot in romance, I had to listen to the pragmatic advice I was hearing everywhere.

I had aesthetic reasons, too. Amish Romance allowed me to pursue story settings that I liked, stories with a nineteenth-century feel to them: limited use of phones, lots of letters, bumpy stagecoach scenes. And also because it was in the country and literally dark or candlelit a lot of the time, it felt more hospitable to the gothic elements I was into.

But the real reason I was writing Amish Romance was that it forced me to stay emotionally honest. Though it was a full-fledged, independent category, Amish Romance still tended toward the Inspirational genre, or even the more general Sweet Romance. Since I suffered, in my life and writing, from an inability to openly and unironically acknowledge emotions, perhaps I ought to choose the subgenre that demanded it.

I'd gotten better at grasping the form. I was getting the rules down, and felt more comfortable with the winding-country-road contours of the genre. But as I grew more literate and discerning, the more I realized that form wasn't the reason my stories still were not quite working. I had studied my Pamela Regis rules closely. If I hadn't quite mastered them, I was still able to deploy them passably well. I could do the dance steps. But dance steps are not the dance. The heartbeat was missing.

While I worked on the problem of the missing heart, I decided to write around it in a kind of literalist gothic way. After getting some positive feedback from my writing group about my buried-alive scene, I'd gone back to read some of Poe's grave-risers. I learned that this story scenario wasn't something that Poe invented—being buried alive was apparently something that people in that period actually worried about. It was possible, in a time in which death was declared based on imprecise heart monitoring, to misdiagnose someone as dead based on a very slow beating heart. It was a very rare condition, but possible.

Writers like Poe and others of that period retailed stories on the subject because live-burial anxiety was already a cultural fixation. In the early nineteenth century, there was a cottage industry of companies marketing signal systems that could be operated from *within a grave*—just in case you accidentally buried your loved one alive. If you were a living person accidentally buried, you could simply pull a lever from within the casket that would raise a signal flag outside the tomb. Some tried to patent this technology.

Accidental live burial, it suddenly occurred to me, could be a good match for an Amish story. The premise was still preposterous, but slightly more believable in this genre.

The part that wouldn't be preposterous, though, was the love story itself. It was based on a real couple. When I lived in Philadelphia I spent a lot of time at Reading Terminal Market, in downtown Philly, which had a sizable Amish presence, including an Amish-run diner that closed on Sunday, missing one of the busiest brunch runs of the week because it was the Lord's Day. One afternoon I'd noticed a young Amish guy heavily flirting with a young non-Amish woman, a local Philly punk. I watched them chat, on and off, all day long, whenever he could sneak away from his work at the diner. And then I saw them do this the next day. And the next. They were truly getting to know each other. She was coming around the diner specifically to see him. It was a real relationship of some kind.

What were they saying? Where did this relationship go? Where *could* it go? I never found out any details, of course. But I thought of these two often. And writing a love story about them felt true to me. When I turned to romance, I knew, even before I'd known about the Amish genre, that I wanted to write about them. And it seemed like a lucky turn for me, as a writer, that one of the main characters was non-Amish, and that much of the setting would be in urban Philly—more solid ground for me as a storyteller.

So there it was. My romance told of the love between one Joseph Young, an Amish man from Central Pennsylvania, a laborer who dreamed of having his own dairy farm in Iowa or Wisconsin, and April, a troubled young punk from Philly who worked at a downtown bakery. They meet at Reading Terminal Market, at the intersection of the Amish-run diner and the bakery. It worked. Maybe the live burial subplot could work, too. Still, I knew, the heartbeat was missing.

My writing group was opening my eyes not just to new genres, but to entirely new modes of storytelling. Janna educated me about the world of fan fiction. Most of what she'd written for our group contained large elements of fanfic, she told me.

"Really," I said to her, "your stories don't sound like fanfic. They're really good."

I immediately realized what a rude thing I'd said. I tried to recover by saying, "Well, I mean, I obviously don't know *anything* about fanfic, but . . ."

Janna was unperturbed.

"Don't worry," she said, "I'm not offended. I get that a lot. And anyway, you clearly *do* like fanfic, because you like my stories, and my stories are all fanfic. So I got news for you: you like fanfic."

Janna was one of the most omnivorous readers I'd ever met. She read everything. In the span of, say, a year, she would read what seemed like an entire genre, then she would write entire fanfic *epics* in that genre. "I don't think you can really understand a genre, how it works, why it works, until you've written fanfic in it," she told me. "That's the whole thing about fanfic."

In the past few years, she'd gotten back into Paranormal. "I like to go with the fads, with what's new, because that's where you're gonna find the best stuff." Sure, this means she reads a lot of boring Paranormal, but it also means she finds a lot of the freshest work in the field, and there's always a sense of excitement in that for her.

"I'm a scientist," Janna told me. She worked in a biotech lab in Boston. "People in my workplace are always reading the latest papers in the field. They have to. The latest articles build on what came before—it's always building on earlier work. You cite what came before you. Reading the newest fanfic can be like that. It's building on what came before, trying to push it a bit further . . . fanfic feels experimental, like science, and that's probably the biggest appeal of it to me."

Janna got her start as a romance reader by reading LGBT stories. "Today, you can do LGBT Paranormal or LGBT Urban Contemporary or LGBT Western, or LGBT Historical. Anything. But back in those days, LGBT *was* the subgenre," she told me. There were scant offerings. When she was just a kid, maybe thirteen years old, she recalled being "desperate for anything even remotely queer. Obviously I was looking for L stuff, especially for gay black women, but it seemed easier to find books about gay white men, so I had to make do with that," she told me, with a laugh. "You work with what you've got."

This was also the reason she'd begun writing fanfic. "I'm not sure whether I knew it was even called 'fanfic' at first. To me, it wasn't like this specialized activity or something. It was just filling the gaps—the, you know, *huge* gaps—that existed in genres I was most interested in. The stuff I was reading was great, but it was missing the elements I was dying to see. So I just scribbled them in myself, in the margins, basically. It just felt like a natural thing to do. And when I found other people, I'm talking now about gay women, who had been doing this, too, well, I knew I had to meet *those* people." Eventually she, like many, found her way to fanfic.net.

It occurred to me that, years earlier, I'd written some fanfic romance myself, just for fun, but never published it. A queer fanfic romance, no less. Like many readers, I'd noticed that there was already a pretty amazing homoerotic romance embedded into the story of *Moby-Dick*. The first 135 pages of the novel, a novella-sized chunk of the story, involved the romance between Ishmael and Queequeg, the harpooner. They share a bed together for a night. "Upon waking next morning about daylight," Ishmael recalled, "I found Queequeg's arm thrown over me in the most loving and affectionate manner. You had almost thought I had been his wife." Before their ship embarks on its epic and fateful voyage, they spend some very meaningful time together in New Bedford. The later loss of Queequeg, thus, takes on a more tragic personal element for Ishmael, which is doubly poignant because it's not quite stated in the story.

For my story, I tried to dig into that part of the book. I imagined Ishmael and Queequeg deciding *not* to board the ship, after all. Instead of sailing the world, on Captain Ahab's pointless and brutal whale hunt, they opted to run away together, west, to California, ostensibly for gold—it was 1850, after all—but also just to be together in a society that was, they'd heard, more permissive than New England. In the end, they move to San Francisco together, and live in a cute bungalow in what is today the Marina district. I'd written a fanfic HEA long before I knew what that was. Though it's not really fanfic until it's shared with the fandom. This step, I would learn, was critical.

Fanfic was about more than dorkish fun. Among the romance fandoms, there are some important ideological conflicts. Some fanfic communities were still reeling from the enormous popularity of *Fifty Shades*, which emerged directly out of the *Twilight* fandom, or, as it is called, the Twifandom. There was controversy at every stage of that history, starting with the decision to "pull to publish"—that is, to pull the story from its free, open-sourced platform on fanfic.net, the place where it first rose to hit status, and to rebrand it into a book on the market, with a price tag. The postpublication bonanza of *Fifty Shades* brought a wave of raiders from the publishing industry who tried to ransack various fandoms in the hopes of finding the Next Big Thing, the next romance gold rush. For many in the fanfic community, this violated their methods and their cherished principles and their space. For those who were more openly left, politically, this was a top-down corporate-capitalist raid on a horizontal anarchist space. Or, as Janna put it to me, "deeply not cool."

Before it was called *Fifty Shades of Grey,* the story, as posted on fanfic.net, was called *Master of the Universe,* or MotU. Before E. L. James was E. L. James, she'd published under the name Snowqueens Icedragon. But around the fandom she was commonly known as Icy. The work of scholars like Anne Jamison has done much to shed light on this history, including the preservation of some fascinating archival documents from that era, such as Icy's (in retrospect) prophetic text chats with Angst Goddess003, the well-known fanfic writer and guru. Like so many others, Icy had read and admired Angst Goddess003's four *Twilight* fan-fiction works, notably *Wide Awake* (WA). AngstGoddess003 had gained a certain sage-like status within the fandom, not only for her fiction work, but for her vigorous articulations about what fanfic was, and, especially, what it was not. The fandom's purpose, to her, was to maintain a space for storytelling that stood apart from capitalist transactions, that was first and last an exercise in egalitarian sharing. Fanfic was supposed to be a place of equal and mutual exchange, in which the currency, available to *all,* was stories, and only stories.

Making a profit wasn't just wrong, it was totally antithetical to the aspirations of fanfic. As AngstGoddess003 also pointed out, profiting by fanfic was also probably a violation of intellectual property laws.

But Icy had big plans. In a text conversation snippet, long since removed from the forum, and later shared by Angst Goddess003 herself, Icy had said, "well don't tell anyone—I have visions of being interviewed by Time Magazine for revolutionizing publishing." This was before MotU became *Fifty Shades* and grossed $200 million in a single year.

Icy asked AngstGoddess003 what she would do should her own fanfic work, the much-loved *Wide Awake*, ever cross over and become a hit in the marketplace. "So if harpercollins came to you and said we would like to publish WA would you say no."

AngstGoddess003 replied: "i would say fuck no." To this, the future E. L. James had said, "hmmm—I'm not sure if I would have that resolve.... unlikely to happen though ..."

"i just get the feeling you don't really.... care about the fandom as a community whole. which is your choice, totally," AngstGoddess003 said at one point.

At another point, Icy quipped, "I'm sure it's easier to take [negativity from fans] with a big fat paycheck LOL."

AngstGoddess003 had responded to that comment by saying, "negativity has its place. it's what stops us all from monopolizing on ideas that arent totally ours."

The political and economic debates around fanfic and romance were far more provocative than I, at that point, had grasped. They got at the basic question of what stories are for—how they are shared, for what reasons, and what that all means, especially in a capitalist society.

To AngstGoddess003, and her school of thought, there was a radical potential in the fanfic form, especially within superpopular fandoms like romance. But to Icy, fandom was always a group of consumers for her product and not an actual community. To her credit, she'd always been clear about her goal to get paid and in a very big way. (The more remarkable fact is that Stephenie Meyer, the author of *Twilight*, never sued E. L. James for infringement.) The ideological debates rage on as both economies, fanfic and romance, continue to grow in tandem, though not always in harmony.

For me, however, the dive into fandom was critical to my education as a romance reader and writer. I immediately recognized the powerfully vital, folk nature of fanfic, an impression that only deepened with time. It made me realize that in a capitalist society, the Great Author, the solitary genius, was just another libertarian racket, wherein everyone is lured by the promise of success but, in reality, only a few individuals have any chance to advance—and when they do, it's winner-takes-all, to the detriment of everyone else. Fanfic, and genre literature, and romance especially, opened up new possibilities, a different kind of literary practice based on a different politics. The conversation happening in those circles was far more progressive and creative and ethically serious than anything I'd seen in the awards-and-grants world of literary publishing, where liberal back-patting replaces serious thinking about the underlying structures of our storytelling culture.

But, of course, I am a product of that culture, too. And as much as I liked to think that I was a hardcore egalitarian, a socialist or maybe even anarchist romancer, like the great Angst Goddess003, I'm sure I probably had some Icy in me, as well.

There is no way of talking about romance without eventually talking about money and its discontents. Ex-ghostwriter Tina had told me that "each one of those books was a stack of bills," which struck me as a precise comparison: mass-market paperbacks and stacks of printed bills are, structurally speaking, almost identical.

Ebooks took off mostly because of romance readers. When I was breaking into romance, the Amazon platform, Kindle Unlimited (KU), had become the latest marketplace. This KU was not a happy place. Rare was the romance author I spoke to about KU who didn't express serious reservations, including those who were doing rather well there. ("Yeah, today I'm doing great," one author told me, "and tomorrow Amazon changes the rules, and my entire business plan is out the window. They hold too many cards.")

Amazon's grip on romance is ever tightening (a sinister combination of words, if ever there was one). Even romance cover art is now governed by Amazon's arbitrary guidelines. They draw the line on forbidden skin strictly if that body belongs to a woman, and more strictly than the previous romance industry standard. Romance cover artists can show you the exact point on a female torso or neckline that will get an author banned from Amazon, measurements that simply don't apply to the male form. And getting banned from Amazon, for breaking their robot-enforced modesty codes, is a status that is hard to undo; getting suddenly shut out of Amazon's platform is a catastrophe for a romance author, especially smaller ones. Few will risk it. And so Amazon rules by fear. It is a perfect example of how a female-dominated field, a genre of stories by and for women, is subject to the whims of a misogynist overlord.

But when I entered the scene, the big battles were raging over Kindle Unlimited's payout situation, the author money. From the readers' perspective, KU offered a pretty good deal: a reader paid $8.99 a month for a subscription and could read as much as she wanted, hence "unlimited." This platform was perfectly designed for romance readers, who read more in two weeks than many people read in a decade.

In theory, the KU platform was also workable for authors of romance. Independent authors, from novices to some of the biggest names in the industry, could circulate their stories directly to readers anywhere—they could even revive old books from their backlists. One big condition for authors: once signed up, a book was to be sold exclusively on the KU platform. And, as usual, authors earned a percentage of sales. If you made the bestseller list, KU's "All-Star" list, your sales jumped (which on Amazon meant an exponential jump). How Amazon programmed this bestseller list became the all-important question.

On the KU platform, the metric for success was determined in terms of page counts. The more page counts your book got, the closer you got to the coveted All-Star list. People also began to discover what it actually meant to land on that list. It was reported that a person could walk away with $50k *a month*. Some people made a lot of money. Some got rich.

Things on KU moved quickly, and because of that speed, it was unclear to many whether changes were for the good or bad. Then, in a short time, it became menacingly clear: there was rampant cheating on the KU platform.

People had managed to manipulate the page-count algorithm. You could produce a "book," stuff it massively with pages, sometimes far more pages than a normal volume, and then program legions of bots to "read" those pages, over and over and over again, as bots can do. The kind of reading done by these bots happens at a different speed and scale than even the most dedicated human reader can achieve. (Were those bots absorbing the drama or emotions of the stories? Probably not— though time will tell.)

Additionally concerning: portions of those stories were being plagiarized. These products, in some cases, were simply giant piles of recycled or stolen romance copy, cobbled together and collated.

Meanwhile, actual authors, including those who'd been pushed off that top-tier list, watched in utter amazement and deepening horror. According to the payout structure of KU: when authors bought into the platform they agreed to a winner-takes-all model, in which authors were in direct competition with one another. Kindle had turned author fees into a zero-sum game. If one person got a hundred thousand percent more page views than you, it meant you made proportionally that much less. There was no rising tide to lift all boats.

The conflict also threatened to turn well-intentioned authors against one another. During the Kindle Unlimited war, some writers wanted to expose these problems in public, often by going to the press and by taking activist stances, hiring lawyers, and demanding additional protections. History has shown that the only factor that forces Amazon's hand is bad media coverage. Others feared such a campaign, for the same reason a worker who toils on a factory floor doesn't want to stand up to a powerful boss.

The writers who struggled the most on the KU platform also feared this battle most. One of these writers told me that she simply couldn't afford to see her product suffer any further. Bad PR for the KU platform would, in her view, simply mean even fewer readers for her.

I'd heard about authors whose finances were severely damaged by this trend. It caused very real hardships for authors who were family breadwinners, managing debt and child care. Everyone knew it was a volatile market, but, still, nobody had expected this type of criminal gaming to take over so quickly. People were scared. And yet many were even more scared to openly question the KU format. Working within Amazon was unavoidable. "All of my books this year are locked into KU," an author told me. "And you know how that goes, it means they are exclusive [to KU]. It's make-or-break for those books, so I need KU to stay up and running."

The authors who took up arms to fight were often the more successful, those who could afford to consider abandoning the platform—they had a cushion of privilege to land on. Amazon kept a close watch on this upper-middle class of high-selling, actual human authors: should they leave KU, especially en masse, it could damage or even bring down the platform. Their continued patronage, lending their trusted author names to the Amazon brand, legitimized the whole enterprise. But most in this class never planned to muster their power—they, too, wanted to stay. Even with the tempest brewing, most expected to continue to work with Amazon.

Matters were made considerably worse because the cheaters also mixed standard publishing techniques into their deceptions. They used pen names, for instance—perfectly legitimate tools of romance trade, but, in this case, deployed expressly to deceive. This, too, caused rifts among legit authors.

At one point romance author, activist, and industry leader Courtney Milan tweeted to her tens of thousands of followers, calling out specific people as scammers. One author, who wasn't one of Milan's targets, replied in a post: "it terrifies me to see this." Milan admitted that she had no concrete evidence, only strong suspicions. But someone needed to take charge.

Writers at the lower end of the market, those struggling most with sales on KU—the kind of writer who launches new brands under new pen names—felt most nervous watching Milan's doxxing campaign. Some of those writers admitted that they needed to do a better job managing their fictional author personas—some confessed that they'd been lazy in grabbing stock images for author photos, for instance—but this didn't mean that they were scammers. On the contrary, many were idealistic and hardworking aspiring writers.

Milan, who is an ex-attorney, was sufficiently aware of the minefield she'd entered by calling out authors by name. But she pointed out that it was very unlikely that she would accidentally call out a poor struggling writer—her campaign concerned those who were succeeding, and in suspicious ways. Nevertheless, others—Milan's followers, for example—might not be as cautious as she. Or, worse, they might weaponize this tactic and intentionally target a competitor. This, at least, was the fear.

Amazon knew that if this platform destroyed actual romance authorship, if this game devolved into an outright scheme, they could be held legally liable. And if human readers and authors, the people who bought into the platform, lost faith, they would abandon it. They had to do something, at least for the sake of appearances. So Amazon sued some of the worst offenders, the ones running the bots. And they changed some of their policies. But I haven't met any romance writers who believe that the new policies go far enough. Most laughed at me when I asked.

Amazon's only real interest in tamping down these schemes was the preservation of the platform. And the platform seems solid for now. In fact, the scammers, by making big gains, may have attracted more people to it—at least in the short term. Amazon, like every tech behemoth, does a gentle slow dance with its most unscrupulous clients.

Even if KU were better regulated, it would still drive significant wealth to a few and leave the vast majority of writers with nothing. Amazon doesn't care who grabs the occasional $10 million payday any more than a casino cares who wins a given jackpot. In the long run, House Always Wins. And, like a casino, Amazon knows that news of big cash prizes entices more people to pay to play the game. As long as their bad press remained mostly under the radar, the game continued.

In the meantime, many authors, from many backgrounds, were fighting these conditions. Most were just fighting to survive. The RWA helped somewhat, but much more organizing would need to happen to mount an effective counterattack. There was a labor war brewing in romance.

But those large, raging battles seemed far away from the battles of my local writing group. On the homefront, in fact, all seemed to be going well until the fifth or sixth meeting. That's when everything changed, and nothing would ever be the same again. No one would dispute that the group's history can be divided into two eras: Pre-Linda2 and Post-Linda2. That, I believe, is the only point of agreement regarding Linda2.

Let me just say, for the record: I really liked Linda2. I liked her the moment she walked in the door. The first impression Linda2 made was that she was remarkably, almost implausibly, old. Later I would come to believe that she conveniently exaggerated her elderness to achieve desired effects—namely, the license to say whatever she pleased and to pretend she didn't hear the responses. The closest she would come to telling us her age was when she said, somewhat cryptically, to the other Linda, "Remember Franklin Delano Roosevelt? Well, that's all I'm saying about *that*." On another occasion, she'd tell me, "Believe me, I'm older than your sweet old gran." This was how Linda2 sometimes talked.

There would be all kinds of rumors about Linda2. That Linda wasn't her real name. That she'd dated Johnny Carson. That she'd been some kind of terrorist briefly in the late '60s. That she'd been a famous romance author back in the '80s. (Naturally, I thought about Tina, the ghostwriter, and how she used to join book clubs without revealing her true identity.) But all of that talk would come later. On that first day, she just gave the impression of being a very old person, who'd arrived only minutes before the class was over, possibly a random confused bystander off the street who'd accidentally stumbled into the wrong place.

Watching her traverse the room had all the allure of watching something important happening in slow motion. Given the amount of time that passed, the members of the group could not possibly refrain from exchanging looks. The first hints of Linda2's sheer Linda2-ness were revealed when Linda1 had exclaimed, "Oh, let me help you," jumped out of her seat, and approached the newcomer. In response, Linda2 shuffled faster and positively swatted her away—and not even like someone shooing a fly but like someone taking a forceful swing at a purse-snatcher. The people who didn't giggle at this, in retrospect, were probably the same people who would never fully warm to Linda2.

Refusing to take any of the closer seats that were offered, Linda2 insisted on trekking to an open seat at the far end of the table. Along the way, she would clutch the back of each chair she passed, to give herself some extra leverage. When she reached my seat, she grasped onto my shoulder instead and gave it a little squeeze. Finally she reached her desired spot, collapsed into it, crossed her legs like a trucker, gave her ankle a little massage, and exclaimed, "Jesus, Mary, and *Jo*seph."

Before anyone had a chance to say anything, she thumbed the room's attention over toward me and said, "What's he doing here?"

This got a big laugh. And it told everyone that this newcomer knew exactly where she was. The old woman, energized by the laughter, suddenly perked up.

"Take a look at this kid. Hasn't eaten in two months." And then, turning to me, she added, "Have a hot dog, kiddo. It won't kill you. Hey, I'm just kidding. Don't worry. We'll be gentle with you."

Linda2, as we would soon find out, liked to talk in the first-person collective. Sometimes it was clear who the "we" were, sometimes it was not. But later that week, there would be some speculation that when she said things like "We had different ideas about how to do this back then," the "we" she meant was Harlequin, where, it was rumored, she'd been an editor. When I probed about her alleged Harlequin past, she just laughed it off.

I presented a convenient target for Linda2. She would say something crazy like, "I've been all around this great big stinking world . . . ," then catch my incredulous gaze, smile, and add, with supreme condescension, "Don't look so excited, kiddo."

One thing was entirely clear to me about Linda2. I was very lucky she hadn't been in this group during the first few sessions, when I'd been handing in my weakest work. If I'd shown those first, fledgling stories to Linda2, it would have been mayhem.

As the group neared what would be its last three meetings, the delicate balance of power began to slip. In fact, a crisis was brewing. Our schedule had been structured in three parts. One: revising old stories. Two: writing new stories, in any subgenre. And, for the third and last period of time: we would all write stories in the same, single subgenre of the group's choosing.

According to the philosophy of our joint leaders, it was essential that, during these last weeks, everyone in the group write in the same subgenre. This would allow us to work better together as a group. It didn't matter what subgenre—it could be Contemporary, Erotic, Historical, or Paranormal. It could be Medical or Amish, though those were not likely. Since it was crucial to this exercise that we all agree, a vote became necessary.

First came the primaries. That was the easy part. Anyone who'd paid any attention to the conversations knew the leading candidates. In one camp there was a marked tendency toward the gothic and the shapeshifting, a taste for subjects equal parts Queer and queer. This group, which tended to the younger side, were fans of the Paranormal genre. Everyone else, generally older and more mainline and whiter, were fans of Historical. In total, we were seven.

Why not allow for both genres? Why not write stories set in Regency England, say, but that also included vampires? Wasn't this broad enough? The Paranormal people exchanged nods with one another.

"That seems fair," Aparna, the Paranormalist leader, said.

"That's not *really* Historical," Janice said. "But we can discuss it."

Linda2, however, had already heard enough.

"Absolutely not," she announced. "I'm not writing about vampires, no no no *no*."

Whether or not all Historicalists agreed with this hardline position, they seemed curious how it would play out. None criticized or offered to amend the Linda2 Doctrine. They adopted it through their silence and they didn't break ranks.

"Well, I think vampires are more of a . . . *specific taste,*" Linda1 said, diplomatically. "But Historical can be set anywhere."

Some of the Paranormalists rolled their eyes.

"You all do know," Janna said, in a tone of uncharacteristic annoyance, "you can write Paranormal stories that don't have vampires in them, right?"

"I'm *not* writing about . . . ," Linda2 said, and then clenched her teeth, apparently too disgusted to even utter the next word, ". . . *creatures*. Or robots. Or werewolves! Or any loser who has fur growing on their palms. What's wrong with real men?"

"A lot," one of the Paranormalists muttered. And another Paranormalist: "And not all romance involves men."

Linda2 either couldn't or didn't want to hear these replies. The room got silent for a long moment. From Aparna's direction, vapor swirled wildly.

The meeting ended with the debate still open. The question would be resolved with a simple vote—but not yet. In what I would come to realize was a shrewd procedural maneuver, Janice moved to delay until the next meeting. "To give us time to think this over without any peer pressure." It sounded reasonable enough to me.

But after Janice adjourned the meeting and I had time to think about it, the situation began to clarify itself. The electoral math was interesting. Linda2's arrival in the group had been divisive socially. She could be domineering and disruptive. She smoked gross cheap cigarettes. Even when she didn't say anything, her moods and silent judgments could greatly alter the dynamic of the conversation. Nevertheless, she was a Historicalist, and this was welcome news to the Historicalists. Her arrival had brought that minority faction into parity with the Paranormalist faction.

Was that the reason she'd mysteriously appeared in the group to begin with? Was she a plant? Maybe she'd been invited by a Historicalist for precisely this reason: to maintain their grip on power. Was this crazy talk? I was once accused, by name, in *The New York Times Magazine*, of having "paranoid thoughts." Maybe I was imagining it.

The Historicalist party, in any case, now had three solid members, Janice and the two Lindas. The Paranormalists were Aparna, Heather, and Janna. In this contest between the two factions, in other words, I would have the deciding vote.

Which was why Linda1's motion to delay the vote, to "give us time to think this over without any peer pressure" had the exact opposite effect. This, I believe, was the intention. Nobody's vote really hung in the balance—except mine. From the recent drift of my stories, Linda1 must have correctly surmised that my vote for Historical could not be relied on, but that it might be coaxed. And so the next few days would be dedicated to one thing: putting peer pressure on me. As someone who already felt like the group's extra wheel, this was exactly not the position I'd wanted to be in.

I woke up the next morning with a text from Linda1. She'd sent it to me at 6:45 a.m.

Have you thought about the big vote? ☺☺

I'm not sure yet, I wrote.

Immediately, she replied.

Oh good! Good to keep an open mind ☺

She added: **Are you leaning Paranormal. Ok if I ask?**

Yeah it's fine. That's correct.

That's why you should vote Historical! Get out of your comfort zone, expand your horizons. Better to write what is harder for you.

Clever, I thought.

Think about it. But it's your decision!! she said.

Would it be terrible if I just abstain? I wrote. **It'll be a tie. And then we could just flip a coin or something?**

To this suggestion, Linda, just wrote **LOL**.

For good measure, she included an emoji of a head spinning in sheer amusement. But I hadn't been kidding. This decision was stressing me out. I didn't want to cast the deciding vote, thus compromising my delicately extended invitation into this group.

But Linda1 was right. Better to anger some and win over others than to make everyone lose respect for me, which is what an abstention would do. And it was also true that these women spent quite a bit of time and mental energy imagining stories about decisive characters, people of action—heroes, we called them, after all—and that abstaining from a vote was a less-than-heroic performance.

Over the course of that day I could sense a slow drip of cowardice draining my resolve. And then Janna, one of the Paranormalists, texted me.

heyyya u votin paranorms??

I def want to, I replied.

FOLLOW YURRR ♥

The next meeting came. It was time to vote. With a shaking voice and a spineless apology, I cast my ballot.

Paranormal, I said, in a grave whisper.

The decision, which had been met either with mild irritation, among the Historical faction, or else with mild excitement, by the Paranormalists, appeared to be, to the group generally, a matter of shared indifference. This surprised me. I'd thought everyone else was stressing as much as I had been. Even Linda2 sat quietly, clearly annoyed but not terribly moved. Everyone seemed already over it. And so we pressed on.

Not I. This campaign and the final vote had been a critical moment for me. Choosing Paranormal felt like a big deal somehow. It felt like I was making a statement about my feelings about love. Namely, that love is weird. Very weird. It's so weird that the only way to honestly and accurately portray it, the only way to tell a realistic story about love, was to include truly odd elements in it: monsters, dark magic, painfully unexplained and deeply unsettling transformations of body and mind. A vampire love tale was the opposite of an escapist story, it was a no-escape story. Maybe that was the essence of love? But whatever the decision meant for me, it was made. And now the question was why, and what next.

Later, when I shared my insights about the Paranormal with Janna, she seemed very amused.

"I'm glad you figured out how horrifying love is," she said, "but you do know that most women learn this by age fourteen, right?"

It was my love for the Paranormal genre of romance, now made official, that ultimately clarified everything. Paranormal, for me, was the control group. For whatever no doubt darkly psychological reasons, my attraction to the Paranormal genre was real, and it wasn't going anywhere. Long before I knew what it was called, I'd liked it. And the more I learned about it, its history and its conventions, the more interested I became in it. Gothic looks at *everything*, plus the things you haven't yet thought of.

So that much was clear. And it was this clarity, this sincere devotion to Paranormal Romance, that made my unexpected flirtation with the Amish genre stand out. If I was so taken by Paranormal, and if every story I was writing at this time bent toward the uncanny, if I had cast my vote for Paranormal, what was the deal with my pull in this other direction? Why was I so excited about something so manifestly hokey as Sweet Romance? What factor could explain this detour into the woodstove aromaed lands of the Amish Romance? The answer was obvious: I was in love.

I hadn't been this happy in love in a long while. It had been years since I'd felt this hopeful about love and relationships. Things with Ania were good. My friends were saying "You seem good" in a way that told me how very not good I'd seemed until then.

"I was kind of worried about you," one of my friends told me. "It was getting kind of dark there for a while."

This was a common sentiment among my friends. But all of this new optimism was getting me concerned. I knew it couldn't last, because Ania and I didn't want the same things. I was not ready to commit to having children. It was, for me, a familiar position: to be happy in a relationship that seemed to have no possible future. It was the kind of relationship about which my therapist would ask, "Is that *why* you're happy, *because* it has no future?" I didn't think so. To me it was about loving our time together and having lots of oxytocin-fueled bonding.

But it was hard to deny that I often did pursue relationships that didn't seem plausible long-term. And so I was feeling a bit doomed, a feeling that was only exacerbated by all the gothic lit I was reading and by the fact that my girlfriend herself was a scholar of Slavic literature, so full of gloomy stories.

Things would have to end sometime, and possibly sooner rather than later. That we were both getting pretty attached was reason to end things, not to remain. The sooner, the better. So counseled her friends, and my friends, too, especially women. As one of my female friends put it, "She wants to have a baby? Yeah, you need to end it. Just leave this poor woman alone already."

In the meantime, we had a basic understanding that we'd

probably break up when she got an academic job somewhere, likely in some small town in a faraway state. That would be it for us. End of story.

Until you have the ending, you can't really know what kind of story you're in. And not knowing what kind of story you're in is the essence of the Barrier. The Barrier was one of Pamela Regis's Eight Essential Elements of Romance. The characters hit barriers that are truly insurmountable. In old-time romances, these were often familial barriers, because of arranged matches, or they were geographical, and required a knight to quest forth and, in those cases, possibly engage in some light warfare. After Jane Austen, it was still warfare, but the conflict happened on the battlefield of social mores. Today, all of the old factors are still there, war and mores, but it's just as often a psychological story, an inner quest of the hero and heroine. This is certainly true in the Gothic, and in Paranormal, where shapeshifting bodies or strange bends of natural law make barriers arise almost anywhere.

But it can take many forms. In some contemporary romance, it's PTSD in soldiers returning from war. It's the violent ex who won't go away. It's the various wounds, exacerbated by the patriarchy, that make messes of our lives. It could even just be your garden-variety divorced douchebag. But for the romance story to work, the relationship needs to read as fundamentally impossible.

Author and RT organizer Tere Michaels had described this to me as the "make-or-break moment—not just to the romance couple themselves, but in the *reader's* experience of reading the romance. It's when the reader also gives up hope. If the reader gives up hope at that point, too, that's when you, as an author, have got a powerful story."

And another thing, Michaels had added. In her experience, the Barrier works best when the author, the person who supposedly holds the power to shape the story, has herself really and truly given up all hope.

I heard this from other authors, too. One author told me, "I always, always reach a point when the love seems completely untenable. I give up, I really do. But then I ask myself: Is this impossible because it really is impossible, or is there a way? Sometimes there is no way, and I trash the story. But when there is a way, I write it." And that is romance. Impossibility is what makes love not just possible but necessary. It's what makes the genre work.

But this wasn't genre lit. It was my life. Or maybe it was a genre called Real Life. In any case, it was *my* real life, and in this version, I didn't have a publisher who'd already sunk a chunk of cash into a series, nor an art team with half-done cover designs, waiting for me to turn in my HEA, per our signed contract. In my real story, there might not be an HEA.

Maybe my story belonged to another genre altogether. Maybe it was, in the end, one of those novels of "literary fiction" that I'd spent my life taking so seriously. Maybe this part of my life was a wistful and wised-up tale of bitter disappointment, with whiffs of larger cultural and sociopolitical malaise. Maybe this would be another Serious Novel about how, in Our Day, in this late-capitalistic hellhole we have entered, where the twentieth-century postmodern prophecies of no truth and no narrator and no reliable witness have finally come to pass, when human life on earth faces extinction, what else can the two parties do but acknowledge that relationships, much less couplings, are now null and void?

I must confess, a part of me believes these things. I have a Thomas Pynchon tattoo on my wrist. I will always be a brainwashed lit major who reads midcentury novels of paranoia with great interest, and who thinks that Foucault had a point. So maybe there really are reasons to believe that Love was a decaying bourgeois ideology. Maybe that's all there was to it? Sometimes the Barrier, like the closed gate in front of the Law, in Kafka's parable, the gate that exists just for you even though it is also locked to you, is all there is. If love and relationships were dead, maybe the only novel fit to print was the one that delivered this sad but true bit of news, ideally with a satisfyingly elegiac ending.

But, as I was learning from my new genre reading and writing, there was other news, too. Literary fiction didn't have a monopoly on hopelessness. Misery was also critical to romance. And *that* gave me hope. Maybe my friends' giving up hope for my relationship meant that there was some hope for me. Misery can be just misery or it could be a sign you're in a romance.

"You feel exposed talking about love," Aparna, fearless co-leader of my romance writing group, had said to me, through a series of short puffs of vapor. She'd tactfully said this to me in private, after the meeting had adjourned. What struck me about her statement was that it wasn't a question. It was, to her, an observed fact, based on my own work. I knew, right away, that she was right. I'd been writing some ridiculous fabley travesties, some decently competent smut. I was mostly just producing a goofy pack of lies. I'd felt exposed right there, on the spot, even when she'd said that.

For me, the experience of writing about love, or talking about it, was like wearing every single item of clothing I owned all at once. Every shirt, every pair of pants, sock, glove, tie, belt, scarf, and boxer brief. Wrapping myself absurdly in all of that, plus maybe grabbing a few other items nearby. The fear of being exposed was met by the desire to cloak myself with everything in my closet.

But Ania was special to me. Early on in our relationship, she'd shared her drawings of enigmatic creatures, like a species of outer-space fox that lived on some kind of ethereal plane. These creatures' deeply soulful eyes were the very same deeply soulful eyes as those of their creator, the same sleepy eyes that I loved looking at and being seen by.

Ania boasted that she alone knew the secret parts of my face. "Well," she conceded. "Me and maybe some other ladies." But before I could ask what she meant, she was stroking the space between my eyebrows. The unibrow. "Nobody can see it because it's so light," she said. "But it's *there* and it's *mine*."

These kinds of statements terrified and thrilled me. This same person would occasionally do mysterious things like decide to make last-minute plans to jaunt away and join a circus in St. Petersburg. It would be a collaboration with Bread and Puppet theater and a Russian circus. During her time there, she represented the circus at a Russian home for cognitively impaired people, talking to the residents about the circus's inclusive performances. Many of the residents had been drawing as she talked, and because she wasn't used to communicating like that, without eye contact, she hadn't been sure they were listening to her presentation. Afterward, however, they lined up to meet her and to touch her fabulously banana-curled hair. (I could relate, as I was myself very much missing those curls while she was away.)

Her version of that day touched me deeply. At some point, a resident of the home approached her and, with quivering hands, grasped hers in his, and confided in her how scared he was. He was in his twenties, he'd explained, but was convinced he would die at age thirty-four, and leave his aging mother alone. He'd been very impressed, he said, by Ania's presentation about her circus. When he said this he was literally shaking in fear and sadness because he wanted to know, he said, if she could tell the future. He needed to know if his mother would be okay when he was gone.

When she told me this story, I thought and felt many kinds of heartbreak for this poor man. But I also felt love for Ania. I could understand why that man had thought she might tell fortunes. She had a power about her that I was constantly aware of while in the presence of her green eyes. I often wondered, *Who is this person?*

Whoever she was, I wanted to be near her. I wanted to glue our heads together with oxytocin. The more time we'd spent together, the more I came to love and need the rhythm of our days. I loved reading essays she was writing about the Literature of the Absurd, and tagging along on her quests, and trying to pronounce Russian words under her forceful tutorials.

I liked helping her scheme career moves. And hearing about secret poems she was writing about shoplifting or snacks. I liked hearing my Slavic diminutive, Aviček, which was often the only word I could understand when she spoke in rapid Russian with her mother, and to which my ears always perked up, like a dog's when it hears its own name.

I felt attached to her hair and her clothes. I liked that she was always on the cusp of changing up her entire wardrobe. And I liked to watch her get dressed. I liked to see her put on her dark turquoise sweater, old and beat-up, with a high neck—that she wore at the angle of innate stylishness—atop a pleated plaid mini, black tights with small polka dots, and what looked to me like ballet shoes with non-ballet soles. I liked the way she noticed me noticing and said, "You should have a scene in your porno when Joseph watches April get dressed and realizes she has a complex inner life."

"It's not a porno, it's a romance," I replied. But she ignored me as she applied eyeliner.

Even before the writers' group officially disbanded, it was clear that the thread had come undone when Aparna suddenly announced that she was quitting. She claimed she had too much work to do. Nobody said it, but the decision to see the *Fifty Shades* movie together was doubling as a kind of graduation rite for us, as a group. I don't remember who proposed seeing it. It's likely that nobody had. It was just collectively and implicitly understood that we would be watching this movie as a group.

That's why I was upset for being excluded on the texts. I would hear people whispering about the *Fifty Shades* outing, alluding to texts that had been sent, texts that I had not received. I also sensed that they were whispering because of me. The message, it seemed, was perfectly clear: they were planning to see this movie without me.

I could empathize. They had been very gracious to accept me, as a straight white dude, into their romance writing group. But there were limits to that invitation. I should respect their decision, as a group, to make this outing exclusive. But because we'd spent so much time talking about *Fifty Shades* and such, and especially because it seemed to be a graduation-y kind of thing, I did feel a bit left out. I'd been seeing ads for *Fifty Shades* all over town and, each time, feeling just a tad wistful about my romance writing group.

I also was somewhat relieved. If I often felt like the odd man of this group, then awkwardly tagging along with them at a Loews theater, to watch this movie, would only make it official. This was, probably, for the best.

I made other plans. On the day of the *Fifty Shades* screening, a Friday night, I would stay home and pity myself while making lentil soup. I noticed the hands of the clock slowly approaching 9:35, the time I'd heard them whispering about. The women were probably already in their seats, waiting for the previews to begin. *What were they talking about?* I wondered. Maybe they were talking about how much they hated me.

Just then, I got a text.

Heyy where are u??

It was Janna.

I know where you are, I replied.

are you joining us?

Was she kidding? This was *all* I wanted.

oh tbh didn't think i was invited 🙂

There was a pause.

HAHA just told everyone what you just said + they can't stop laughing.

And then she added: **of course you're invited.**

As I'd later found out, my number and Janna's had been accidentally left off the group texts. Unlike me, Janna had simply asked to be included.

it hasn't started yet. get over here!!!!!

So I ran over to the theater, and missed very little of the action. When I got there the women were still laughing at me. The movie was okay. Dakota Johnson was impressive, especially considering the movie's overall problems. The Christian Grey character was weak. He had the body of an underwear model but the charm of an iguana. It didn't much matter. For me the best part of the movie was after the credits rolled, when the group reconvened at a bar across the street and began to unpack the whole thing together.

They also checked in with one another—one person in the group was in mourning for her father, another had been dealing with a recent medical crisis. People in the group asked for updates, and gave help to one another in a variety of ways. This would be our last meeting.

"Don't listen to him," Aparna said of one of my comments on the movie, "he's been brainwashed by Amish Romance."

At one point, when some of the genre questions started to get a bit speculative, and elaborate, Janna pulled out a notebook.

"Here's how I would have done it," she said, and began scribbling down the names of each character. Together we helped her turn a movie of a book—a book that had been fanfic of another book—back into a work of fanfic. We stayed there for hours, laughing and drinking, until closing time.

Months later, on a night of falling stars, I drove down to the southern end of Cape Cod, with Ania and her sister, Asya, and a friend, Vera. We'd all been excited by the last-second stargazing excursion to watch what was going to be an unusually spectacular meteor shower. As usual, we fed off Asya's high energy. She'd spent the car ride excitedly reading aloud from articles about the meteors.

It was thrilling, when we reached the coast, to finally see the big black field where these wild creatures lived. We'd pulled up to the shoreline, where the Atlantic lapped gently, right on the edge of the entire continent, and where the water, in the other direction, stretched out coldly and effortlessly to an infinite black horizon, the biggest theater conceivable. The theater that night was electric with anticipation.

The show itself offered one gentle explosion after another. And there was no stinginess about this meteor shower: it was a fireworks show. Every few seconds we'd see a popper or a runner. And every few minutes there would be a major arrival, a diva of fire skating on ice, at a somehow leisurely and ostentatious pace, trailing a showy tail of sequins and feathers that you could almost hear rustling by.

When we'd first arrived, a layer of homes along the shore

served as a buffer, blocking our access. But as soon as we found a path to the beach, around the homes, Asya took to a full run. I considered, for a moment, that she would simply continue running, and do a swan dive into the black water. Vera, laughing, followed her. We could hear their voices, insistent and loud, but softened by the giant ocean sky. Soon Asya was literally jumping up and down, farther along the beach, pointing to a certain meteor, to get us to look at it. Twenty seconds later, I saw her and Vera, on a rocky patch at the edge of the water, looking for the perfect boulder on which to recline and watch the meteors.

Ania took my hand and drew me close. I smiled at the familiar feel of her small, strong body against mine.

"You're just cuddling because you're cold," I said to her.

This was a running semi-joke between us. She'd told me early on in our relationship that her ideal mate was something she described as a "man blanket."

"So what," she said, and pushed me to walk forward.

The truth was that I liked the role.

We walked toward the water, pulling at each other every few seconds to gesture at a shooting star the other had just missed. At first, I'd been a cold pragmatist about our stargazing. I would look in the opposite direction of where Ania was looking, so that, together, we'd have the sky covered. But then I realized the foolishness of this approach. It wasn't like we were watching for dropping mortar shells. The point wasn't to see everything but to see together.

So I turned to look in the direction she was looking, and at just that moment, a gigantic diva star blazed across her patch of sky. I saw it first over the back of her head and, because she saw it, too, and quickly turned around, eager to tell me, she caught me already looking at her. We had a moment.

I saw her and the meteor at once, streaming over her long curls, just as she said the word "look . . ." And at that moment, I wanted to have a child who looked exactly like her. I loved her. I would be happy to stay together forever. To make a family. To bring a little swaddled, floppy-headed baby to our parents and say, "Meet your grandchild." But I couldn't tell her any of that. Because I wasn't certain yet. And I'd made promises before that I couldn't keep, and that was a dark, sad road for me. I didn't want to do that again.

She gave me a knowing look, and a small curl of the lips. One of the things I really loved about her was how shy she was to say "I love you," which made the times when she mustered it up far more electric and precious. Despite our different views on the world—every time I signed off with "See you later" she would reply, "See you soon"—we had developed a strong ability to communicate nonverbally. Her message to me, telegraphed by her eyes and mouth at that moment, was fully legible. And for that same reason, I also immediately sought to shut down the emotion on both sides. I prepared to say something intentionally really dumb. The dumber and more transparently intentional, the better.

But I caught myself. I thought about my old romance writing group. We hadn't met in almost a year, but certain statements had stayed with me. Janna's edit on my stories, that I went for a laugh where an emotion should have been. I had tried to remedy that problem in my writing. But I was still struggling to apply this edit to life's actual dialogues. It was still hard for me.

This was a moment to show her, and myself, that I wasn't just dabbling in romance writing, but that I actually got it. This message could take almost any form: from a nonverbal cue, a hand squeeze, to a bolder reply, an *I love you*. Almost anything would be acceptable. And maybe even lovely. Anything would do. So I made a reply.

"That was a *nice* one," I said.

It wasn't the absolute worst thing that could have come out of my mouth. And I'd said it with genuine enthusiasm. I'd tried to give it a specific, warmish tone that conveyed, by implication, that the shooting star's "niceness" was at least partly the result of having seen it together.

But who sees a glorious shooting star at the exact same moment as he sees its reflection in his lover's marvelous hair and feels overwhelmed by love for her and says *That was a* nice *one*? These could only be the words of a divorced douchebag.

I could tell she was disappointed by my comment, which, largely because causing disappointment was its intent, only made me sad for us both. And somehow more sad because the hint of that disappointment was just that, a hint: she wasn't allowing herself to get dragged down by it. She was, in general, in that period, rolling with me in these moments, being, as they say, a good sport.

"I should put that in the book," I suddenly heard myself saying, and immediately profoundly regretted it.

"The porno?" Ania said, ever the good sport. She lifted her gaze back to the sky and its meteors.

"Yeah, that one," I replied. "The romance."

She nodded vaguely, and turned to watch the part of the sky where I wasn't looking.

We didn't see much of each other for the rest of the week. She was too busy, she said, dealing with roommate drama, and working on applications for jobs—jobs that would take her far away.

PART THREE

The Little Mermaid

The point of ritual death. The point of ritual death marks the moment in the narrative when the union between heroine and hero, the hoped-for resolution, seems absolutely impossible, when it seems that the barrier will remain, more substantial than ever. The happy ending is most in jeopardy at this point.

—PAMELA REGIS, *A NATURAL HISTORY OF THE ROMANCE NOVEL*

During this period, while my girlfriend was mostly avoiding me, I made a decision. I would commit to cross-genre: Amish and Gothic. It would officially be Amish Romantic Suspense. Why choose just one? Better to mix it up. I was already getting some positive feedback on my bonnet ripper (in which, incidentally, no bonnets are harmed, except one that's carried away by a squirrel, in what becomes a small but critical turn in the story), but I knew I had to have some gothic elements in there, too. It was not common to create cross-genre hybrids between an Inspirational subgenre (e.g., Amish Romance) and Suspense, and it was even less common to cross the Suspense genre with Inspirational via Amish. And yet, at that time, Amish Romantic Suspense, though uncommon, was not unheard of.

I was encouraged to learn that Harlequin was publishing a quiet series of Amish Romantic Suspense. My interpretation: this was a small field, but promising. Maybe it would grow, maybe not. But there was just enough possibility, and few enough people already doing it, that there was hope. This was the time to jump in.

My setting would be half in Philly, half in the Amish areas west of Philly. There would be a kidnapping, a live burial, and a panicked unburial. That would be the suspense plot. It made my heart race just to think of how terrifying a live burial would actually feel for the people involved. Planning for this scene, I'd recently come across a recording from an old RWA conference for a panel discussion titled "Dead Right Autopsies for Authors."

"Corpses pop up everywhere," read the description of the session, "from family funerals to violent crimes to creatures that won't stay buried. This workshop introduces authors to the specifics of the postmortem from time of death estimates to Y-incisions. Get the facts for your fiction—we'll cover it all from cadaver to slab!"

I learned much from this session. And I was grateful that I could listen to the recording instead of being there in person as the one male in a hotel conference room for a session on dissecting corpses. It also reassured me that my genre research interests were valid, and not merely creepy, even if they were also that. But of course the story I was writing would be about love, and how love cannot be buried, and will not be killed. There would be no overt mentions of vampires or such, but they would be there, too, on the edges, as they always are, if you're really being realistic.

"Um, *no*?" Nellie had said to me, when I mentioned Amish Romantic Suspense to her. "Honestly, I don't think this would work. People who read Amish are looking for sweet. This is way too fucked-up and dark."

Seeing that I felt let down by her reply, she went further. "And *especially* coming from some creepy-ass *dude*. I knew you were a perv."

But Nellie knew the deal: with romance, anything is possible. Naysayers are always on the wrong side of romance history. I'd once dated an editor who worked for a non-romance imprint at a major publishing house, where she had a great track record acquiring fiction titles. But she'd made one major romance error that she would carry with her to the grave: she'd passed on *Fifty Shades* when it had landed on her desk, back in '09. She told me this as we lay in bed. I mentioned the irony that she was interested in domination in her real life, but had still passed on *Fifty Shades*.

"I *know*," she said, glumly. "But I thought it was just awful."

Nellie worked in the romance business, and she knew never to say never. And so, despite her well-founded hesitations about my proposal for Amish Romantic Suspense, she added, "But, yeah, you know, *someone* out there will be into it. Go for it."

She advised me to publish it with one of the small imprints— some of which were independent outfits, some attached to large publishers—that specialized in mash-ups. Her own publisher had just such an outfit, located down the hall from her. It was a kind of fiction lab, designed to cultivate the next genre-making big seller.

"It's wild times over there," she told me of this experimental imprint. "They're up for anything."

We walked over from Nellie's office. I met an editor, who had pinkish hair that perfectly matched the tone of her pink glasses' frames. She told me that they accepted manuscripts from authors with or without agents. They published roughly twenty titles a month—digital only. But the goal was to cultivate new authors and bring them into more lucrative markets. Fantasy readers, she told me, are particularly fond of the old-style hardcover book. "They like that *object*," she said.

Nellie, who was standing there with me, said, "Tell him about the dolphin sex book."

"Well, it's shapeshiftery," the editor corrected her. "But yes, it is a dolphin."

"Who knows," Nellie said, "could be the next thing."

When we returned to Nellie's office, I told her that I hadn't given up my Amish hopes just yet. I mentioned Harlequin's Amish Romantic Suspense series. It was category: Inspirational, part of their Love Inspired line, in the Suspense genre. The tagline was "Amish Country Danger." It was about a formerly Amish woman, Heather Miller, who returns to Amish country to reopen a B&B. Heather is trying to put her life together after her ex-husband, and dangerous stalker, has finally been put away for the murder of another of his exes. But when he escapes, and immediately finds her at the Amish-country B&B, things get scary. Which is why it's good that U.S. Marshal Zachary Walker, who has his own painful connections to this escaped killer, is sent to protect her. Heather and Zachary have a wild adventure together and, under the worst of circumstances, fall in love. As luck would have it, I happened to have a copy of *Plain Sanctuary* by Alison Stone on me. I dove into my bag, which was resting against Nellie's desk, and pulled the book out.

"Lemme see that," Nellie said, waving her hand impatiently at me.

I handed it to her. She studied the cover. A blue and brooding storm envelops the farm. There are no human figures visible, only a big scary house, with vague sources of illumination within, an open window rattling in the wind, and a horseless buggy abandoned in front of a cavernous barn. A bolt of lightning can be seen in the sky. It was a romance book but with a solidly gothic cover image.

"Hmm," Nellie said. "Interesting. Well. Give it a shot, I guess?"

My heart leapt. Was Nellie actually encouraging me? Sensing my hope rising, she immediately snapped back.

"Yeah, but you're still a creepy-ass dude," she said.

"But you really think I have a shot?" I replied.

"I dunno," Nellie said absently, with a shrug, as she turned back to her desktop to reply to pressing messages.

So I did my homework. My grasp of the romance mechanics had gotten tight. True, the suspense/thriller element was a bit new to me, but it was close enough to Paranormal and old Gothic that I felt like I was in familiar territory.

I also went deeper into the Amish genre. I did a lot of research on everything about Amish life in Pennsylvania, especially among those Amish who work in Philly's marketplaces. The Amish I had grown up near in Ohio came from a different community than those in the eastern part of Pennsylvania. One community referred to non-Amish people as "Yankees" and another as "Englishers." There were other differences in dialect, dress, religious practice, and social mores. Unlike the neighboring Amish of my youth, where people attached orange reflective triangles for safety to their buggies, some outlier communities outlawed the practice as too modern. This religious debate felt familiar to me. I interviewed as many people as I could, from various regions, including Michigan and Iowa.

I also took advantage of my magazine assignment travel to do research. On an Amtrak train across New York State, I sat next to a twenty-one-year-old Amish man. As it turned out, he knew some of the same Amish families I knew from my childhood summer-camp years in western Pennsylvania. We chatted for more than two hours. My romance hero was, in some general way, derived from this real-life young man.

He told me about a country song he'd heard once—and only once. It had happened in a Home Depot, where he was tagging along on a lumber pickup. He'd loved that song, he told me, but he had never even known its name. I was struck by the poetry of that, of being able to hear a song on the radio only if heard by accident in a Home Depot. Of loving a song and never being able to hear it again.

Naturally I'd pressed him for some remembered lyrics. It was, he told me, "something about a man from Louisiana and a woman from Mississippi. Or maybe the other way around." I looked it up and discovered that it was "Louisiana Woman, Mississippi Man," a duet by Conway Twitty and Loretta Lynn.

I asked him if it was okay for me to play it for him. He said it was. And so, for two minutes, this young Amish guy and I leaned in close to my phone, as the train barreled through darkening rural landscapes, listening to this charming song together. It was a lovely and touching moment. Obviously that scene migrated directly into my romance in progress. Except that instead of me, some chatty divorced guy bothering him on the train, the role of song-sharer is played by my heroine, April, a punk from North Philly.

It was a nice scene in the romance. But, still, scenes like that were pushing me toward a genre problem. I was bending some rules of the Amish Romance genre, at least in its more conservative form: 1) the love affair should not involve an Amish with a non-Amish person (unless the non-Amish becomes Amish), 2) the story should be set in a rural Amish area, and 3) no explicit sex or drinking or drugs. But I could address these violations by having April join an Amish community at the end of the story, as part of the HEA, and also by taking the story from Philly into the countryside by at least the middle of the first book of the series, and leaving it out there, in the woods and fields. As for all of the hot sex and bong hits I'd already begun sketching out for this tale, I'd just have to cut those.

Ania was mad that I was cutting out the sex scenes. "So you're really not doing pornos?" she had asked, dejectedly.

Some of my leftist comrades would see these moves as a capitulation to reactionary forces within romance. Even though I'd hedged myself into a corner here with a fairly conservative genre whose readership skewed heavily to Christian or "traditional" values, my friends had a point. I decided I could stop short of having April going fully Christian at the end. I would try to tiptoe this storyline in the plot, so that it didn't read like Jesus propaganda, but also stay true enough to the genre.

Owning the genre hybrid would also help, letting the dark and gothic elements unsettle anything too comfortably inspirational. And, as a bonus, it would make the book marketable to Paranormal and Suspense readers. The gothic mystery would come courtesy of the sudden disappearance of April's sister, Rose (named after Pete Rose, a nice Philly touch, I thought). She is also a punk. The hunt for Rose is what brings Joseph into April's life at first, until, bizarrely, the desperate and increasingly mysterious search for Rose darkly intersects with their budding but tenuous romance. Eventually April thinks she has to choose between her new lover and her lost sister.

I won't give away the ending. But it's a mixed bag, HEA-wise, because this story is only book one in the series. In technical romance lingo, it's more of HFN (Happy for Now). Ups and downs will drive book two, and things get more openly paranormal as we discover that Rose, when she was buried alive in the first book, gained some powers of unusual perception.

All of that technical, story-craft stuff was going well. But the heartbeat was still inaudible. Maybe it wasn't there at all? This was a serious writing problem. I was coming to understand that the story would not work, and would not sell to a publisher, if it was emotionally disingenuous. It had to be real. I needed to open myself up for this one. That was going to be "the challenge of this book," according to my therapist. "And by 'book,'" she continued, "I mean 'your life, right now.'"

At first, I argued with my therapist about that interpretation. By professional obligation, she wasn't going to argue back, except to nod smugly and raise her eyebrow, to communicate, as only a therapist can, that I was growing defensive at her provocation, which meant, without a doubt, that I was completely wrong and she was completely right.

It didn't take long for life to catch up to her prediction. After some quick progress with the Amish Romantic Suspense, followed by months of stagnation, I was beginning to fear that I was writing pointlessly. As a result, I hesitated to submit my work to publishers. I was coming to realize that the whole sincerity-in-love thing, the parts where I dealt with my own scary and real vulnerabilities, was indeed the challenge of this book, which is to say, my life at that moment.

My relationship with Ania was only getting better and thus worse. Rapidly approaching was the day of decision: whether we would have a future together, and, if so, what kind. In the meantime, we could just enjoy being together. And then suddenly that changed. Even as I toiled over my romance, a very romance-novel thing happened: we found out that she was pregnant.

But this was not a romance novel. There was no guarantee that it would end well. Maybe this wasn't a barrier to overcome, but a barrier that you don't: an unhappy ending. I'd had some of those. I knew what they looked like, and this looked like that.

Immediately we shifted gears from our happy-but-doomed status quo into crisis mode. It was decision time about us. And the decision was higher stakes than we'd planned for.

She had discovered her pregnancy when she was abroad, on her trip to Russia, when she had temporarily joined the circus, mostly as a researcher. One of the child performers in that circus had, somewhat spookily, asked her when her baby was coming, even though it was only weeks into the pregnancy, and she wasn't showing at all, and wasn't even certain she was pregnant. But once confirmed, she realized that the signs were there: that the impulsive trip to join a St. Petersburg circus was itself one of her indicators of pregnancy.

When she returned, we had the most difficult and strained weeks of our relationship. We did, however, get off to a positive start by deciding to try couple's therapy. And we also knew just who the therapist would be: a person whose couch we'd bought off Craigslist.

Months earlier, we'd shown up at her office near Central Square in Cambridge, Massachusetts, with a hired truck. We'd gone from calling her "the couch woman" to, once we'd chatted with her, "the couple's therapist with the couch." Back in those happier times, the entire scenario was amusing. It was funny that we were buying a tear-stained therapist's couch to help Ania's sister furnish her new home. As we'd hauled it away, we'd jokingly—but quite seriously, since we knew we were doomed—told the therapist, as we stood under the hot summer sun, that we might see her again, in her professional capacity, soon enough.

Now, months later, as fall arrived, that day had come. With the surprise pregnancy, and plenty to discuss, we knew we had the number to call. When we showed up to our first session, I tried to break the ice by saying, "So . . . how's the new couch been treating you?"

Through many painful conversations we reached a conclusion to abort and to try again later in the year, to give ourselves, our careers, and our relationship time to grow into that moment with intention and planning. The conversations had been stressful for both of us. At various points we very nearly broke up. There were days when I went to sleep thinking that we were going to say goodbye to each other forever.

But the opposite happened. We came out with a more secure understanding. And we'd reached this understanding because we trusted each other. That itself felt like a test we had passed. We made the decision to stay together, to move somewhere together, and to try for a baby in the future together. We were a team.

But on the morning of the abortion, we were a million miles apart. I watched her, in a quiet and resolute attitude, listening to moody songs from The National as she ate her organic toaster strudel, dressed herself in plaids, and applied her makeup. In the Lyft, on the way to Planned Parenthood, we held hands. But we were in our own bubbles.

"You're upbeat," she said, wearily, as I sang quietly along to Queen in the car.

I was clearly behaving inappropriately. It was nervous energy. But, I have to confess, I *was* feeling upbeat. I was proud that we were doing this together, and that we were on the same page, for once, about the future. I did, however, take her note and ceased from singing "Bohemian Rhapsody," to be more present, and especially to be more present for the one who was going through far more than I was that day.

We held hands as we walked past a gaunt woman in stained jeans handing out antiabortion flyers outside the fortresslike clinic on Commonwealth Ave, until a clinic worker intercepted us, to help usher us in. The security checkpoint at Planned Parenthood is not a matter of routine. It is alive with a very real sense of menace. The vigilance and anxiety there reminded me of war zones that I'd been in. Once inside, though, the clinic was nothing like that.

There was a kindness, a feeling of empowerment and hope freely and generously given to all who entered. And many did, from all walks of life, to receive many kinds of treatments. It helped that the TV ran cheerful daytime programming, sound muted. A buoyant musical soundtrack streamed from speakers. At points this created some strange moments for me: for instance, when "Shake It Off" by Taylor Swift played. But the calming effect was achieved. Aside from swirling emotions about why we were here, my anxiety in that place was mostly about the security measures I had seen outside, and the reasons for those measures. A determined person with an AR-15 could probably get into this building. I tried not to think about it. I noticed a woman reading a Linda Lael Miller romance. Based on her delighted reactions to the book, it seemed a companionable volume. It was good to see the HEA here.

A language barrier suddenly opened up between Ania and me. While we waited, she identified emotions she was feeling that were, she said, indescribable in the English language. Russian was necessary to capture these particular feelings.

And there was one issue we hadn't fully discussed. Ania and I, it turned out, may have fundamentally disagreed about whether an early-term fetus has a soul. This disagreement, or possibly misunderstanding, about the ontology of fetuses' possible souls, though bad, is surely worse when discussed for the first time in a Planned Parenthood waiting room. Worse yet if this arguably important conversation happens literally seconds before the examination.

Ania, leaning her head on my shoulder, sighed. Then she whispered, "This poor ten-week fetus's soul . . ." She wasn't putting forth an argument. It was just a lament. She certainly wasn't asking for my comment. But it alarmed me.

"Do you really think that?" I asked. "You think there's a soul there?"

She nodded.

I didn't know how to reply.

"Maybe we shouldn't . . . be here?" I finally said.

"You *don't* believe it has a soul?" she asked.

"No," I said. "I mean, I dunno. I can't say I *do* believe that."

In the very next beat, a nurse wearing pink scrubs called Ania's name. I was dumbfounded. I watched her jump up and walk directly toward the nurse, and disappear without turning back.

Later, when Ania gave me the full report, she'd told me that, despite our joint decision, she had, in fact, committed herself to making a final decision on her own, only once she was in the examination room.

In that room, things had gotten more complicated, but also more simple. Since she hadn't yet undergone a prenatal exam, that day's scans were a first look. And what they showed was a nonviable pregnancy that could not have come to term. The pregnancy would have been terminated anyway, probably by miscarriage. It made our decision to have a child later, in the future, feel more validated.

I experienced these dramas, of tests and anxious anticipation from the waiting room, where occasionally Ania would run out to give me plot-twisting updates. Which included some distressing thoughts.

"It might not be your fault," she said, breathlessly, at one point, of the non-forming fetus.

"Oh," I said.

"It might be *my* fault. Or no one's fault. There's a one-in-four chance."

She'd begun to worry that she hadn't been eating well enough. Maybe she should eat meat? More folic acid? Finally we realized we didn't need to solve this mystery right now. And we sat still, holding each other, cycling through sadness and relief and sheer adrenaline.

The night before the exam, we'd sat on her couch, eating her customary gummy bears and tea, and going down a list, issue by issue, planning a future, and a future family together: the terms of cohabiting, of potentially living a nomadic academic life, of speaking Russian with kids, of public schools, parental involvements, Jew stuff, socialism.

That's when she had told me that she would probably mourn. Possibly she would get a tattoo of currants and lingonberries.

"To mark your experience?" I'd asked.

"No," she said, laughing. "That's very American of you."

"So what's the idea?"

"It's going to be a ghost for me," she said. "That's how it is for some women. They stay with us, as ghosts, for our whole lives."

"*They*," I murmured.

"Scared?" she said.

I nodded.

"It's not really a scary kind of thing for us," she said. "But it is a presence."

Months earlier, before the pregnancy, before we'd fully discussed us, we'd each individually made our decisions about this relationship. Mine had come at the Copenhagen airport, Kastrup—which reminded me of Hans Castorp from Thomas Mann's *The Magic Mountain*—where I was laid over for a day on my way back from the Arctic. I'd been traveling for a magazine article on NASA's airborne survey, Operation IceBridge, based in Kangerlussuaq, Greenland. It had been a tiring couple of weeks, but, for me, a life-changing experience to see the true north, to see, from impossible angles, the 100,000-year-old polar ice cap, and the retreating glaciers. I also witnessed the politically fraught and the deeply anxious NASA climate science data-gathering operation.

While in the Arctic, I had also done a surprising amount of romance writing, in between interviews and transcribing notes. On the long transits over the ice, while sleeping NASA crew members reclined in every nook of the crowded plane, like cats, I'd taken out my notebook to work on my Amish Romance. There was something weirdly clarifying about gliding a mere 1,500 feet over the frozen world of the north. Flying that low, at an altitude ideal for NASA's laser and lidar data-gathering equipment to survey the terrain, created a variety of strange effects on me. It often felt as though we were skimming along the surface.

I was reading Igloolik literature and I'd met with a local shaman and historian. I had also read as much as I could of the science and journalism about the polar regions. But of course my mind also drifted to Mary Shelley, who'd brought her monster to ruin in the Arctic.

"I am an abortion," says the nameless creature of *Frankenstein* before drifting off on a raft of ice. That's how the monster's story ends.

Shelley's monster can be read as a story of the author's own tenuous position in society, as a woman who is expected to create life constantly—Shelley had been serially pregnant in the period when she wrote *Frankenstein*—but whose body betrays her and whose talent and ambition and hopes can only come back to haunt her. All stories emerge from the real-life struggles of their authors. You don't necessarily need to know about them to appreciate the work, but once you do know of those struggles, it's hard to read the stories any other way.

The vastness of the Arctic landscape, and the ancient cold, created the conditions for a deep and primal intimacy—a fact confirmed by the forlorn and lonely NASA folks I traveled with. The proximity of another person, the desire to huddle together for warmth, was essential. In such a place, I could imagine people falling in love.

I sketched out a scene in my book, in which the lovers—the Amish man, Joseph, and the Philly punk, April—their forbidden love thwarted almost everywhere else, set out on a sleigh ride into the frozen wilds of wintry Pennsylvania. This was exactly one of the reasons I'd chosen to write an Amish book. It gave me an excuse to write scenes like this. Joseph and his brothers had been building a new house, in preparation for his sister and new brother-in-law, who would arrive that spring. Until then, the house sat empty. Joseph makes an excuse to go there, to do repairs. It wasn't a lie. Joseph would, in fact, do some repairs (which was also an excuse for me to describe him hotly laboring in front of her). So Joseph and April take a bus to Lancaster one evening, then jump on a horse and sleigh, and gallop over snow-covered cornfields, their first time truly alone. Their plan is simple: one night at the cabin, and then they break up. But, for one night, they cast off hopelessness and pretend that this is possible.

I looked out the NASA airplane window and imagined a sleigh flying across that snowy plain below, carrying these two lovers in search of privacy.

April, who's barely ever left the city in her life, is alarmed, and she checks that the runners of the sleigh are still on the ground, and that they aren't in fact flying through the air. In that sleigh they can finally reveal how much they love and need each other, how happy they've been every time they meet, and how much they've lusted after each other's bodies. Needless to say, things got pretty steamy in that sleigh. (A genre-violating turn I would later edit.) And then they arrive, once again at the remote cottage, for some more steamy action that I would later edit. Thus I stumbled on a method to writing romance that lacked sex but not attraction: to write in the sex shamelessly but to cut it later, in the hopes that its echoes remained in the story.

For the first time I could really see how these two people, who should not be together, might, truly, imagine a shared life, if only for a moment. Their joy was palpable to me. And, as the Orion P-3, an old Cold War Navy plane, pushed forward, with a NASA aircraft engineer snoring soundly next to me, I was in tears.

Later, when I was less emotionally raw about it, when the cold-eyed editor in me looked over the pages to assess it, I knew the scene was pretty good. That sleigh ride was the beating heart of this story, the thing I couldn't fake. In my mind, it was the beating heart of my real-life love that had made it possible.

Now I could see this thing as a book with a cover on it. A story that had been fun and liberating to write was now something I could probably publish, a story that a romance reader might be truly moved by if they read it. When I did finally show my work in progress to some book editors, a senior editor at Kensington cited the sleigh scene as the thing that persuaded her.

Everything about my own life at that time had made me lose confidence in my ability to know what was good for me, what would work and what wouldn't. But now I felt like I was passing through that. I had a shot at writing a new narrative.

Aside from personal hesitations, many of which amounted to financial fears, I had also worried about bringing a child into a world that was experiencing the "sixth extinction." My magazine assignment to the Arctic made the predictions about humanity's future on earth more concrete to me. Like many people of my generation, I do the math every time I see those big dates, 2040, 2050. How old will I be when the ice is gone? When the oceans reclaim the coastal cities? When the unfrozen permafrost unleashes its methane? A child of mine could easily live to see 2100. A grandchild of mine could see the world of the twenty-second century. It seemed not only sad but even reckless to create another mouth to feed.

But I'd shifted significantly during my short time in the Arctic. It was hardly clear from this experience that my conclusion should be to have a baby. And yet there was some part of me that couldn't help but want to share the beauty and mysteries of the earth with this young person, precisely because so much of it is slipping away and because our lives here are so precarious.

At the Copenhagen airport on my way home, having logged something like seventy hours of flight time in the past few days, I was dead tired. I awaited another flight, the last leg, to Boston. With my Amish romance on my lap, I awoke in confusion, in front of Hans Christian Andersen's luggage.

Was I dreaming? For a moment, I honestly wasn't certain. Kastrup airport had apparently created a little Hans Christian Andersen exhibit in the middle of the terminal. In my exhaustion, I hadn't noticed that I'd collapsed on a chair right in front of it. Two items were on display: a giant crusty suitcase that once belonged to Andersen, printed with the initials H*C*A— one small brushstroke of paint away from HEA, I noticed— and a small statue representing one of Andersen's best-loved creations, *Den lille Havfrue,* the Little Mermaid. It was the artist Edvard Erikson's original model for the 1913-era version of the life-sized mermaid statue that lives on the shoreline rocks just west of the city center. I'd passed by it the day before and stopped to spend some time there, watching families pose their children, especially their girl children, with that statue.

At the airport, I was more interested in Andersen's old suitcase. I was also, decidedly, in the minority. For a full hour, passenger after passenger stopped by the exhibit, surprised and delighted to find the Little Mermaid where they least expected her. Most people, it seems, really just wanted the story, the stuff of imagination, and they didn't really care about the author. They were, without exception, completely indifferent to his dingy, melancholic luggage.

What was the mermaid to them? Few of the passengers who stopped probably considered the troubling aspects of Andersen's story about a girl whose sole ambition was personhood—an ambition that is brutally thwarted. In a negotiation with the Sea Witch, she agrees to three extreme conditions in exchange for becoming human: first, that she give up her tongue and her sublime singing voice to the witch, and second, that she experience constant, extreme pain in her new feet. Literally every step she took in this world was painful for her (she is also given the gift of being a skilled dancer, but this, to say the least, is more of a curse). And, last, she agrees that, despite the pain, she will wage a campaign to win the love of a certain prince. Should she fail, she would literally melt into oblivion. That was the best deal a mermaid could get on dry land.

The tragedy of the story is that she, in fact, does succeed, and it still isn't enough. After saving the life of the prince, and charming him, she impresses him with her dances at the ball despite the agony. But in the end she is summarily passed over by him, left to await her inevitable punishment.

There is, however, one last offer for her to consider. In exchange for killing the prince, and using his blood to transform herself back into a mermaid, she can resume her previous life underwater with her family and community and, in accordance with the unique biology of mermaids, live for three hundred years under the sea. Out of love and devotion, she refuses, and she dissolves into bubbles on the surface of the sea. Even this act of heroism is anonymous, unrecognized.

The story can be read as the basic conundrum of femininity in society: there is simply no version of a human woman, no body type, no behavior, no talent, that will give a woman access to a normal life. The surprise ending, in which the Little Mermaid is elevated as a kind of saint—after her body is dissolved into mist—seems, to me, like a particularly cruel conclusion, a cold comfort for her exclusion from the physical world, the one she'd been pining for, the one that any of us would pine for.

The good news, I suppose, was that I appeared to be one of the few people in Copenhagen at that moment entertaining such dark musings. After ambushing and informally interviewing a few of the passengers who took selfies with the Little Mermaid statue, it emerged that their version of the story was, of course, shaped by the Disney adaptation, in which Ariel ultimately becomes fully human and, through a series of lucky turns, does marry the prince. In the last scene of that movie, the couple depart together by boat. This HEA is the ending people tend to remember.

But what drew people to the Little Mermaid statue wasn't really the story's plot, much less its ending, either Andersen's or Disney's, but something less verbal and less distinct. They were drawn by something emotional and tonal. They remember the wondrous visions of the undersea world. Just as the mermaid longed for our world, we still long for hers. The busy passengers at Kastrup, for a passing moment, felt a flicker of genuine and unexpected joy amid the existential stress of an airport. Those reactions, the relief, the sudden recognition in their weary faces, was, I had to admit, a very tangible kind of happy ending to the Little Mermaid narrative. It was like watching a three-dimensional fan-fiction forum. Like the masses of "Brokeback Mountain" fans who drove Annie Proulx crazy with their desire for a rewrite, here was another example of people deciding, on their own, what their stories mean to them.

I had my own version, too. Andersen's luggage was triggering me. And yet I'd huddled by it, unable to look away. Its being ignored, even if I could understand why, made me even more sad. The meaning, for me, of the luggage seemed transparent. It was a stand-in for the writer's life, for the anxieties of that life. This luggage didn't have the gloss of immortal literature, but the heaviness of real life. It was what it was: baggage.

And the mermaid? What did she stand in for? Literature? Hopes? Liberation? Love? Delusion? Or maybe just a well-executed example of a human-fish shapeshifting tale?

Therapist Deborah's voice came to me. I imagined the sound of it, the smooth, cold constancy of the humidifier in her office, its spout of water vapor like a dancing soul. She would lead me away from my verbal tricks. I called upon her when I needed her.

In a short time, I'd determined that Hans Christian Andersen's luggage more or less represented depression to me, and the mermaid represented enchantment. *A choice?* I wondered. *Doom or enchantment?*

But I'd been doing my therapy work, and I knew that it wasn't really a choice between the two. It was about trying to embrace both, and each, as permanent pieces of myself, parts of my history, including the painful stuff, so that I could live my life with a bit more hope. So that was the decision, it seemed: to live. To accept the author's luggage, which was beautiful in its way, and also full to the brim with hurt. And, with that luggage, to walk toward the mermaid.

Sitting next to Kastrup airport's Little Mermaid, as she herself sat, pining away, I pulled out my laptop and jumped headlong into a new romance story. My mind buzzed. It would be a shapeshifter, this one. A Little Mermaid fanfic? I hadn't done too much fantasy stuff of late—I had even avoided Viking romance in the Arctic—but I was confident I would do better with it now, with all that had happened. Good fantasy is really hard to do, because if you aren't in control, and precise, and patient in your world-building, it's horrendous to read. But when it is good, it can be very affecting. The Little Mermaid suffered terribly and she deserved better. Shapeshifting was about bodily pain and how it challenges love. Stories featuring disabled characters are becoming bigger in romance. *I should read more of those,* I thought. I furiously sketched out a possible scenario. But then I stopped. Hadn't I, only a minute earlier, made the promise to choose life? I stopped writing romance.

I opened up another document and began a love note to the woman who was waiting for me back across the Atlantic. I told her the truth about how much she had meant to me over the time I'd known her. But just before I could send it to her, I lost juice on the laptop, and before I could find an outlet, it was time to board the plane. When I got back home, I didn't show her what I'd written.

But *I* knew what I'd written in that letter. I'd been thinking it for a while now. And I wouldn't forget it. It only took me six more months, and a fair bit more drama for me to work up the nerve to say it to her face. I wanted to build a life with her. When I got on that plane in Copenhagen, to fly back to her, I knew, without a doubt, that I wanted to try this with her. Technically a 747 had flown me home, but I am certain that I could have made the flight without any plane at all.

I felt the same feeling of elation months later, on the morning of the abortion: that feeling of really being in it together. After leaving Planned Parenthood, we walked on Commonwealth Ave and got pizza. It was a particular kind of New England late-fall sunny day, with bright but heavily angled, not-exactly-warm sunlight merging with shadow to give colors a mellow, darkly salient glow. The city felt quiet and gentle, and I was relieved for that. As we walked, Ania described the experience of the procedure for me, the strange unexpected colors and sounds. It was easier to talk about the sounds than the emotions. What was it like for something to be so consequential but also essentially uneventful? I tried to use my imagination to feel a bit of what she had just gone through.

I thought about the soul Ania had drawn for me, on scrap paper, at the River Gods bar, on our third date. It looked like a psychedelic flowering vagina. And now, years later, the River Gods bar was gone and we were walking out of Planned Parenthood, speaking to each other in hushed tones. What was the meaning of this narrative arc?

In my fixation on the Barrier stage, I'd completely ignored a later step in Pamela Regis's catalog of romance elements: the

Point of Ritual Death. As a gothic reader, I should have been far more aware of it, especially because Ania had strongly hinted at it that night, before the procedure.

It's going to be a ghost for me, she had said. *A presence.*

When she'd told me that, when she'd said she was planning to mourn, I somehow conveniently avoided the implication that I ought to join her. This wasn't just her experience of mourning, it was ours. I needed to work harder to think about what that meant. I needed to get in touch with that presence, too, and to join Ania in this place.

Ritual Death was present, according to Regis, even in contemporary non-Gothic Romance stories, though often masked. It brought death into the story of love, not as a side plot but as the central turning point of the narrative. It was the door that needed to open and then to close for good. It is the story's first ending, the painful and seemingly final ending that must happen before a happy ending can occur. That experience of death is what makes love so urgent and lasting. Ania and I had committed to a happy ending together, but we couldn't reach it until we passed through this. It was important not to skip steps in the story.

And when I thought about it, I had an image of what Ania meant by "a presence." That scene in *I Love Dick,* when Chris Kraus dunks herself in a serene pool with two gorgeous men, who we learn are her two former abortions, apparently two young gallants now—very athletic, almost godly. It's a sad and funny scene. But most striking, to me was its tone, an organic calmness: nothing seems as peaceful and normal to Chris as bathing with her two abortion spirits against the backdrop of a sublime desert plain and mountain-range horizon. It was an image that stayed with me long after I'd finished reading that book. But, still, there was no way I could fully understand Ania's experience.

The closest I could get, probably, was in returning to her phrase, "some women." I remembered other women in my life, and their experiences with abortions and lost pregnancies—and how I probably wasn't there for those women when they'd shared their stories with me, because of how it opened up troubling feelings of my own. I thought about the miscarried fetus my mother once referred to as "the one between Adena and you." My mother had miscarried in a bathroom in a synagogue that overlooked the Old City walls of Jerusalem. She was in that neighborhood to pick up my sister from day care. My mother's reaction, which still surprises her today, was rage.

When she'd emerged from the synagogue, she found a palm tree sapling and fell on it, and with a lot of determined pulling, she managed to rip it clean out of the ground. More than forty years later, the dried, exquisitely layered palm frond still lives in the home of a close family friend. "It's your half-sibling," my mother told me. I suppose I had my own ghosts, too. And even though I knew that story, did I ever mourn with my mother? I didn't. Just as now I hadn't thought about the Ritual Death stage of my relationship, even though I had Regis's catalog of romance elements literally posted on my wall.

It was obvious why I'd ignored it. I may be death-obsessed, but in real life, I'm far less willing or able to deal with it. People close to me have died, including young people, and it's never something I've handled well. Maybe my fixation on literary death is just a way of not dealing with those actual deaths.

But here was an example of Gothic Romance coming through, in a concrete way, and at a difficult moment. And this time I would mourn. It would be painful. It would be an experience of losing control. The Ritual Death phase would throw open the doors to all kind of emotions, and memories of loss from the past. It would force me to confront the recent, unprocessed, and still somewhat traumatic experience of nearly losing this relationship. We would mourn in our own ways. But we would also mourn together, and we would live together with the presence. The story of happiness found, if it is to have any meaning, must live with loss.

The next week, at a bar in Somerville, Ania and I listened to a friend of ours, a philosophy professor, tell us the story of a disheveled philosopher who hadn't noticed that a nest of wasps had taken hold in his office at the university. The nest had remained there for two years.

"They were very *established*," our earnest and very precise philosopher friend said, a few times, of these wasps.

I watched Ania, laughing at the story, and noticing me notice her.

A bit more than a year later, we were living together in Ann Arbor, and I was planning a trip to New York City, for my first RWA conference. I wasn't certain whether I should register under my given name or under Dana Becker, my new pen name. I'd recently signed a two-book deal, with Kensington, for my

Amish Romantic Suspense series, grave-risings and sexy sleigh rides and all. The series had been acquired at a modest advance by a major publisher, which meant that Dana Becker was going to be a bona fide romance brand. Dana Becker was also now a member of the RWA. But the book wasn't out yet. It hadn't even been edited.

I was, in fact, meeting my editor for the first time at that conference. This was a source of some anxiety. My manuscript contained some plot twists that still needed work. I couldn't just glide on the sleigh runners of Sweet Romance for this one. I also hadn't done anything to build a social media presence. Dana Becker had a single follower, @avi_steinberg. Becker still had a lot of work to do, and I was slightly shy to meet the editor of his book. Especially since she was a star in the field of romance. She had witnessed and helped shape every major trend of the post-1972 romance boom.

I was intimidated to meet her partly because of Nellie. Nellie's voice never ceased to haunt me. She knew the business so well, and needless to say she had never believed I'd manage to follow through on my plan to publish a romance novel. When I'd hung out with her at a recent RT conference, Nellie had been astonished to hear that a respected veteran editor was taking my work seriously. I hadn't yet signed the contract, but I was inching tantalizingly close.

"*Really*? The *Amish* one?" she'd said, as we'd walked the halls of the Atlanta Hyatt Regency, en route to one of her pashmina handout–type events. "I mean . . . I didn't *read* it. *Obviously*." (I'd sent her a copy weeks earlier.) This put a smile back on her face. But it faded quickly.

That's when I realized something was weird. Something was happening. In some kind of twitchy, twinkling shimmer of magic, right there in the halls of the Hyatt Regency, I saw it clearly. I realized I was witnessing something I would remember. Nellie, with real, possibly physical reluctance, was working toward something resembling a compliment.

It was going to be a very quick exchange, a flicker and gone forever.

"Wow," Nellie said. "I'm kind of . . . impressed."

And then she caught herself. In the long half-second since she'd allowed the word "impressed" to pass her lips, she'd already walked back the comment.

"I wonder how you'll mess it up," she said. "You know it's not just one book, right? You'd *better* have a series for them. Or they'll eat you alive."

I did have a series for them. Whether I was going to be eaten alive remained to be seen.

"No, it doesn't *'remain to be seen,'*" Nellie had said, with maximal sarcasm, when I'd said those words. "It's going to happen. You're definitely going down. And you're going down even bigger than I realized. This is actually gonna be even better than I thought."

My first meeting with my new Kensington editor went well. It was at the 2019 RWA conference. We went to an expensive Italian place in Midtown, near the conference hotel, the dystopianly vertical Marriott in Times Square. At the restaurant, she had asked for a specific table upstairs that she knew about, which was quieter than the others. Her New York game was strong. Mine was as weak as ever. It had taken me more than one swipe to get my MetroCard to work that morning. I was having trouble positioning my unfashionably clad body in such a way as to not irritate locals. I was more bumpkiny than usual. This is what even one year in Michigan can do to a person. But it was all good. I was Dana Becker now, and Dana Becker, romance author from the Midwest, was, I decided, a charming out-of-towner.

It wasn't difficult to imagine this Dana Becker as a truly new persona. Much had changed for me in the past year. Ania and I got married. We made a little ceremony of it, on our back porch, in the presence of our immediate families and a bunch of flamboyantly colored autumn trees. And by the next year, we had a baby. At the RWA conference, I was a brand-new dad, and had spent my free time in an illegal New York Airbnb trying to catch up on sleep. The meeting with my new romance editor went smoothly because we spent much of it discussing babies.

I talked about the baby a lot at that conference, mostly because people consistently asked me to tell the *whole* story, with pictures. During a lull, sitting around having drinks with some RWA authors, I told them tales of the Labor and Delivery nurse who gave us this advice: when Ania pumps milk, and to help increase volume, she should look at a photo of the baby before and during the "let-down," as the nurse called it. "Helps get those hormone levels to tick up," she'd added, tonelessly, as one does after an exhaustingly busy night shift. Because I was also tired, I couldn't help but laugh at hearing a mother's love framed so unsentimentally, and with such deadpan bureaucratic precision, as a dose of oxytocin you should shoot every two to three hours. The nurse, misinterpreting me, or simply not caring for my sense of humor, replied with unshaken crispness.

"Just give it a shot," she said. "It works."

Ania had told me that, immediately after giving birth, she didn't want to hear any bad news, or read dark stories, or see anything scary on TV. She couldn't even stand to listen to a Nirvana song when it came on the radio. The gothic mode was not going to be helpful for her. She'd read that this postpartum desire for positive stories was typical. Was this it? I asked those romance authors at the bar. Was this the biological basis of the HEA?

As I shared these thoughts, I realized I was behaving somewhat like a rambling new parent, and maybe just a weird rando. I apologized.

"Are you joking?" one author said to me. "This is what I live for."

She wasn't exaggerating. Stories like this were literally her livelihood and vocation. She was thinking of doing a Medical Romance series, she said. "This is research for me." The others agreed. And they weren't merely being polite. They urged me to continue.

"Yeah," said another author, who may have been a bit tipsy at that point. "We want *all* the details. Spill 'em."

In other publishing spaces, telling long stories about your newborn tends to land somewhere on the spectrum between quirkily irrelevant and unforgivably unserious. But at the RWA, if you had a real-life HEA to share, people sincerely wanted to hear about it. With the notable exception of Nellie—whose response to my mentioning the magical birth of my child was, "*Eww*. No. Seriously. Don't even, with me." Even more than my forthcoming debut with Kensington, this enthusiasm for my real-life HEA made me feel at home among the romancers.

"I became a romance writer when I became a mom," one author said to me. "Typical story. Like you!"

"Like *me*?" I'd said.

"Isn't that your story?" she replied. "Became a romance author when you were having a kid?"

I hadn't thought of my path to romance in quite those terms, nor did I see myself as typical in this way, since in nearly every other way I was an atypical romance author. But it was true. I had met so many people, famous and struggling authors alike, who mentioned similar histories. And similar not necessarily in content—having children—but in form. There was the mid-career switch, the post-trauma decision, the postpartum project, the side gig. Making the move to become a romance author often seemed to mean reaching a crossroads in life, where, as one author put it to me, "if I don't do it now, I'll never do it."

Much of that year I'd spent mulling over two new names: my unborn daughter's name and my romance pen name. Dana Becker had been easier to come up with, but the processes had overlapped. Once, when searching for romance books online, to determine whether "Dana Becker" was taken, I had, out of curiosity, searched to see if there were any authors with the name Zoya. What I found immediately is that Danielle Steel published a big, very red, Soviet-set novel called *Zoya*, a nice specimen of a Cold War–era romance. This discovery hardly clinched the name for me, but I also didn't mind this little nod from the romance world.

There were days when I'd toggled between lists of names, one for the new me and one for my child. It felt right to me, this coincidence of new names. It struck me as hopeful, and also a bit funny, which is, in its way, another form of hope.

The highlight of the RWA conference, RITA Awards night, was particularly electric that year. I felt it the moment I got off the endless series of escalators to the hotel ballroom. People who'd been to the event for decades agreed: the air was charged. After a year of open battle—the culmination of a few years of simmering conflicts—the community of romance authors (in their largest official body) was coming together to reaffirm their bonds to one another, or, at least, to test them. In retrospect, it was a brief moment of hope, or maybe a last gasp, before the bottom fell out of the RWA.

The big lingering issue in the RWA, and in the industry generally, was structural racism. Every writer of color had numerous stories of slights and insults, large and small, in the industry. Historical romance author and scholar Piper Huguley had recently shown that the number of black male romance heroes was in decline. She saw no coincidence that her own highest-selling story was also her only interracial romance and that one of her publishers insisted on putting only heroines on the covers of stories involving black men.

The RITA Awards were a case in point: in the RITAs' entire

history, black authors had been not merely underrepresented but entirely shut out—a fact that I continued to re-google because it was so astonishing. The issue had reached such a fevered pitch that the RWA's president had recently claimed that she was ready to discontinue the RITAs if reforms in judging were not implemented immediately. Nobody wanted to see them canceled, so changes were made, and at that evening's gala, four authors of color went home with awards.

But it wasn't enough. Just a few months later, in January 2020, the next RITAs event, scheduled for that summer, was already canceled. The frayed bonds holding together the RWA in 2019 gave way in 2020 because of a full-scale insurgency. It happened on Christmas Eve 2019, when the organization formally suspended one of its own leaders, Courtney Milan. Milan, who is Chinese American, had publicly criticized a decades-old book by a white romance author as a "fucking racist mess" for its depictions of Chinese people and culture. The author of that book had lodged a formal complaint to the RWA's ethics committee—a body that Milan herself had once led—claiming that Milan had damaged her reputation and career. The committee found in the complainant's favor, and instead of addressing the well-founded charges of racism, they suspended the person who spoke out about racism.

Because Milan is a beloved leader in the community, and a respected author, this punishment launched a furious and widespread revolt within the RWA ranks and among its most influential members. It sent the organization into a tailspin. Within days, the leaders responsible for this outrage resigned in disgrace, and those who remained scrambled to clean up the expensive mess. But the damage was done. The major publishers—Harlequin, Avon, Kensington, Penguin Random House, and others—pulled out of the RWA20 conference. Scores of RWA people canceled their memberships.

The damage, in fact, had taken place over decades and decades. The Milan situation was just the final straw. Because she is a powerful person in the field, Milan's case had sent shock waves through romance, but how many writers of color, how many other marginalized authors, had suffered over the years and had their careers stalled, or even ruined, by the entrenched bigotry of the organization? By 2020, the only way forward was through revolution. And the fact that it happened, and so forcefully, proved what romance people had long suspected: The citizens of Romancelandia were better and more powerful than any one institution.

The signs were all there at the RWA conference in 2019. I witnessed it myself. At the general meeting at the start of the conference, the controversies of the past year were discussed using phrases like "need for diversity" and "more inclusivity." The much uglier but more accurate word "racism" was nowhere to be heard, a convenient omission that is, of course, itself a feature of structural racism.

One might have guessed that, in this environment, Brenda Jackson's event during the conference would have been well attended. If her status as a romance legend didn't draw people, perhaps they should have been moved by the constant talk about listening to black authors. The conversation among the mostly black women in that session did not suffer for its small size; it was the white RWA members, who didn't show up, who lost out.

Jackson spoke candidly about race. And unlike some speakers at the awards ceremony later, she cast a critical eye on the term "trailblazer" in reference to her career. She didn't, she said, see herself as breaking any boundaries. On the contrary, the boundaries still exist, and they continue to confine writers of color. She'd won a very lucrative Harlequin contract only once she was a reliable bestseller—they turned her away early in her career. This path didn't exactly throw open the doors of opportunity for others. It didn't prove that these publishers were open to black authors or to black narratives. It proved only that they were open to perennial bestsellers.

Speaking at the RITAs ceremony, LaQuette, a romance author and also the president of the influential New York RWA regional chapter, said, "Readers, look beyond stories not centered on your experience." And then she put it more directly: "You can identify with lions and tigers and bears, why not my narrative?"

It was a stunning remark, a brave humanist stance, that mixed ethical indictment, loving rebuke, and pointed challenge for a ballroom full of her fellow romance authors and industry people. In a genre in which everything is possible, what does it mean that people of color are still routinely denied the basic dignity of telling their story and having another person relate to it? No one who heard what she said, who really heard it, will ever forget it. Months later, during the insurrection, LaQuette would try to stay in the RWA to help right the ship, and when that proved impossible, she resigned.

Between the speeches and awards at the RITAs ceremony, I would check my BabyTracker app. As an official romance author, I suddenly had much business to attend to there. Sessions on marketing and on Amish Romance and Romantic Suspense were suddenly of pragmatic concern, and offered me useful intel, not just casual intrigue. But my mind was back home, with Zoya.

Our newborn was so newly born that we were still tallying up every feeding. This allowed me to indulge my impulse for charts and graphs, but it was also a way to bond with her when we were apart. I could feel my heart beat a bit faster every time I saw that notification that she'd taken another 30–60cc of milk. I knew exactly how she looked when she did it, with her tiny arms locked in a bent position, her tiny fists balled up tightly at her sides like a daredevil poised to make some kind of giant leap. There was so much strength in her tiny body. She was struggling for life in a way that I could barely imagine.

Because she was having trouble breastfeeding in those first weeks, she was bottle-feeding a lot. Secretly, this gave me great joy. It meant that I got to feed her myself, and feeding this child, I'd come to realize, was an overwhelming emotional experience. I certainly hadn't expected that.

There were daily revelations. One morning, I sneezed. I sneeze loudly. That my sneezes are unusually loud is a matter of public record. That same cover article in *The New York Times Magazine*, from a few years ago, in which I was described as having "paranoid thoughts," had also described my sneezes as "echoing terrifyingly." And those particular sneezes weren't even my loudest. But this sneeze was a big one.

Across the room, I heard a plaintive cry issuing out from deep inside the bassinet. It was one of the saddest and funniest moments of my life. This is not an exaggeration. Something hit me: that little tiny person in the bassinet was a separate person of her own. She lived in her own brain and body, and in space. Weeks earlier, she'd been a bump, a hazy image of a toe-tip on a screen, and today she was a human citizen whose autonomy and essential otherness I would have to respect.

And respect was the weird and completely unexpected attitude I already had toward her. And admiration. She was such a hard worker. There was no playtime for her in those first weeks. No hanging out. She was on a mission. Some part of me had already begun preparing for a future in which she would be an adult, and I would have to contend with the usual parental problem of always also seeing her as a child. What I didn't expect, and could not prepare for, was how this projection also worked backward in time: that even during her infancy, I would be contending with her adult presence.

When I heard her cry out, startled by my sneeze, I realized I would never totally understand her, or her subjectivity, and that her life was hers alone. And yet we were so tied together. We would never be neutral to each other. No sneeze would go unnoticed, no audible cry unfelt. Always connected, for the rest of our lives, through invisible strands in the air.

My mother had told me that when I was an infant she'd seen flashes of faces from her dearly departed grandparents in my face. I saw the same thing in this child. A return of ancestors, but just momentarily. They were present in her face even though she didn't really resemble them. She did resemble her mother, though, especially in the little down-curved upper lip. This is exactly what I'd wanted, and yet, when it happened, the intensity of my joy was a surprise.

In the afternoons, Ania's maternal grandmother, Babushka Natasha, would take baby Zoya out for a walk along the Huron River. Grandma Natasha had been visiting us from Chicago. Her role in her grandchildren's lives had been very hands-on, serving as math tutor and teaching all of them to recite from memory, and with proper locution, poems of Pushkin and Mayakovsky—as any well-raised child should. After a day of doing infant care for us, she would sit around and solve calculus equations for fun. She had assigned professions to all of her grandchildren: who was going to be a concert pianist and who was going to be a scholar of Russian literature. She was still waiting for the family mathematician, and she had already begun whispering in her great-granddaughter's tiny ear about it.

As we played with baby Zoya, Babushka Natasha impressed upon me her belief that Tolstoy could recall, in detail, memories from when he was an infant. She believed in genius and in the classics. These days she read mostly Georgette Heyer romances, which are exactly the kind of romance that would appeal to a fan of the classics. On her walks with Zoya, she had a copy of *Arabella* on hand.

For those daily walks, it was my job to prepare the bottle and the various baby-shmattes, carry the bassinet down the steps, and set up the stroller. I loved watching great-grandmother and baby together. Babushka Natasha, born in Odessa during Stalin's reign; and Zoya, who, if she should reach Babushka's age, will see the turn of the twenty-second century. On some day in that twenty-second century, will elder Zoya be found taking out her great-granddaughter for a walk? It was up to her, and to fate. It was a story whose ending I will never know. My job was simply to give her enough bottles to get her further along on that journey. On this day, anyway, those two were gazing into each other's eyes, Babushka Natasha beaming at Zoya, and Zoya beaming right back. Then they were off on their river walk and picnic.

During Babushka Natasha's visit, I couldn't find a book on my shelf. It was *Rasputin and Other Ironies,* a collection of essays by the writer Teffi, who wrote funny gossipy journalism during the late Czarist, early Soviet period. I had a feeling I knew where the book had gone.

Ania had recently mounted an all-out assault on the bookshelves. It happened during the pre-labor phase, the very end of pregnancy, when nesting behaviors take on a feverish pace. I had watched silently, so as not to disturb the pregnant lady in the wild, as Ania did what I had, many times, requested that she not do: alphabetize my books. I like my books to be on the shelf in an order of my own devising, more akin to seating frenemies at a party. This apparent disorganization drove her crazy, and the time had finally come, she believed, to do something about it. We obviously couldn't bring a child into a home marked by such chaos.

And now, weeks later, after we'd brought the baby home, with my books fully alphabetized, I could confidently say that my Teffi book was not in its place, and that it had gone missing.

But I knew where it was. A year earlier, when we had been preparing for our big move west, and for all of the changes that were to come, I had been looking over Ania's shelves of books, at her place in Somerville, feeling sentimental about the paperback classics she had, once upon a time, dutifully collected like a good student of the Great Books program at the University of Chicago. At the time, before alphabetization had become a sticking point between us, I'd also felt touched to see that she'd carefully alphabetized them.

I liked having my own collection. I also really liked her collection—and I doubly liked that it was *hers*, and that I could borrow books from it, and return them to her shelves. Looking at her books was another way to see *her*, and I loved seeing her in all her ways.

I was excited for the move, but anxious. For whatever reason, this anxiety took the form of worrying about my bookshelves. Possibly I was just being a control freak. Possibly I was displacing other fears onto this trivial boundary question. I was also probably feeling insecure about her judgments of some of my books, many of which might be deemed less than serious by University of Chicago standards.

So, that day, I finally just asked her: When we move in together next year, did she want to join our book collections together?

From the other side of the room, she lit up, and walked over to me. "I *really* like that," she said, putting her arms around me and smiling. "That's one of the most romantic things you've ever said to me."

I immediately felt guilty for not saying more romantic things to her. And guiltier, still, because I wasn't even trying to be romantic now, either. I was just being neurotic. But I had to admit, now that she pointed it out, it was a romantic thing to say because it was vulnerable and unguarded. I wasn't going to tell her that, in this instance, my courage was an accident. Instead I smiled and took the credit.

"But," she quickly added, surveying her shelves, "I think we should keep our books separate."

Maybe it was because we'd met in the library. Or maybe it was just because it felt perfectly timed. As I stood in front of her alphabetized shelves, my heart swelled with love knowing that our books would, of course, get all mixed up together.

And now, a bit more than a year later, I drifted over to her shelves, where I found, as I had suspected, my Teffi book. It was naturally in the properly alphabetized spot in her collection. I lifted a hand to retrieve it, but then I stopped, and I left it there, on her shelf.

I wandered into the bedroom. Ania and Zoya and I had had plans to go out that night. But there was a big thunderstorm outside and we would have to wait for the rain to pass. Water and wind thrashed around like thick ropes hitting the starboard side of the house. Our street turned into a rushing river. Lightning was flashing, and thunder was getting louder. It felt both dangerous and cozy. I climbed into bed, where Ania and Zoya lay. We curled up and lay there together, one bed, three hearts, of varying sizes.

Ania and I were wide awake, and the tiny little person between us, who'd gone down to the softest of sleeps, was riding out this angry storm like a dandelion seed safely perched atop a fast-moving river. I listened to her sleeping sounds—which were alternatingly baby-sweet and comically hoglike—and I listened to the rain, and to my love's voice whispering to me, knowing that we would have to leave this bed at some point in our lives, and maybe soon, but not yet.

Right now, this was the only place I needed or wanted to be. "Ever after" was real because it is tangible, not some kind of numb bliss state. It wasn't about being free from pain, but free enough to see something more than pain. And it didn't mean perpetual happiness, but it did mean forever. It was as permanent and unnegotiable as my love for the child sleeping next to me. And it was forever because I could summon up that moment, three hearts in one bed on a rainy evening, and how I felt at that moment, anywhere, anytime, for as long as I have life in me. And I can remind myself, if I ever need reminding, that, yes, I am lucky enough to hold a share in happiness.

Acknowledgments

So many people helped shape this book, directly or indirectly. I feel everlasting gratitude for:

My editors past and present, Ronit Feldman and Dan Meyer. For Nan Talese and Sonny Mehta. For Jennifer Lyons. For Rachel Molland. Dan Novack. For the copyeditors and production people, and for everyone at Doubleday who has helped put this book into the hands of readers.

For Jesse Green. Alexis Coe. Jeff LeBlanc, Sarah LeBlanc. Noam Osband, Devora Keller, Ezra Feldman, Laura Martin. Tovah Day. Rami Cohen. Susan Coyne. Lainie Schultz. Dvora Meyers. Sasha Weiss. Sarah Sonnenfeld. Beverly Schneider. Jesse Kellerman. Seth Wikas. Dee Bigfoot. Augusta Rohrbach. Kamau Parker. Elissa Bell Bayraktar. Dominique Barrault. Kenice Mobley. Marie Jena. Dana Hammer. Alison Hammer and cats Sassy Pot and Beebe and Buster, Seamus Moriarty. For Kayla Rosen, and for Anita Leyfell (1917–2019), a dear friend and inspiration. For all of my teachers.

For Vida Engstrand. Alicia Condon. For Nellie. CJ Hollenbach. Sarah Wendell. Carol Stacy, Tere Michaels and the RT staff. For Tina. For RWA friends, while it lasted; to my secret informants at Harlequin and Avon, and so many others in and around Romancelandia. And, of course, for Jane Austen.

For the people of Annie's Children's center. Sarah Schmidt. The Michigan Society of Fellows and the Residential College at the University of Michigan. For Yaddo. The Harvard and U-M libraries. For all scholars of literary history, and especially for those studying contemporary romance.

For the *mishpocha*. Ima, Aba, Adena, Shay. Irina, Sasha, Asya, and Sam. Babushkas Natasha and Faina. All my family in California and Boston, and between. For Annka. And, for the smallest one of them all, Zoyka!

A NOTE ABOUT THE AUTHOR

Avi Steinberg is the author of *The Lost Book of Mormon* and *Running the Books: The Adventures of an Accidental Prison Librarian*, which was a *San Francisco Chronicle* Best Book of the Year. He is a regular contributor to *The New York Times Magazine* and *The New Yorker*'s Culture Desk blog.

A NOTE ON THE TYPE

This book was set in Adobe Garamond. Designed for the Adobe Corporation by Robert Slimbach, the fonts are based on types first cut by Claude Garamond (ca. 1480–1561). Garamond was a pupil of Geoffroy Tory and is believed to have followed the Venetian models, although he introduced a number of important differences, and it is to him that we owe the letter we now know as "old style."